Maritime Heritage

LIVERPOOL AND THE MERSEY

Volume 1

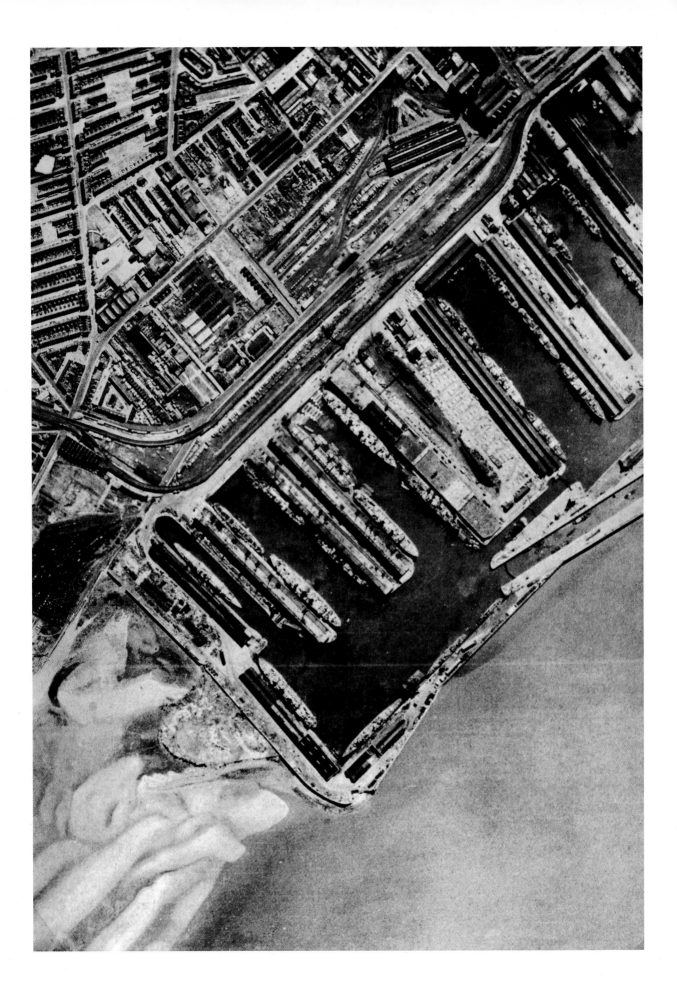

Maritime Heritage

LIVERPOOL AND THE MERSEY

Vol 1: Gladstone Dock and the great liners

Ken Longbottom

Silver Link Publishing Ltd

This volume is dedicated to the late K. C. Crafter and the late W. B. Hallam
who, like myself, were founder members of the Merseyside Branch of the World Ship Society,
and did much to stimulate my interest in the ships of Liverpool and the Mersey.

First published in June 1995

British Library Cataloguing in Publication Data

A catalogue record for this book is available from the British Library.

ISBN 1 85794 053 9

All photographs are from the author's collection unless otherwise credited.

Silver Link Publishing Ltd
Unit 5
Home Farm Close
Church Street
Wadenhoe
Peterborough PE8 5TE
Tel/fax (01832) 720440

Printed and bound in Great Britain

Frontispiece **An aerial view of Gladstone Dock during the Second World War.**

Title page **A view of Gladstone Dock in 1914 taken from the top of the pump house, showing the magnificent stern line of the new** *Aquitania*. **The clean condition of the new dock is also very evident, and with not too much dockside clutter as well. Shades of the commercial artist featured on the cover and page 23!** *C. Heywood*

Opposite **Following the war the dock was fully completed, and the Gladstone Dock Estate was opened by Their Majesties King George V and Queen Mary on 19 July 1927. The Royal Party was carried on the Dock Board's tender** *Galatea*, **seen here steaming through the great lock and about to break the tape, cheered by thousands of spectators.**

ACKNOWLEDGEMENTS

My thanks are due to the following: Mr C. Heywood, for his considerable assistance in the preparation of this volume; Mr H. Leadbetter, for proofreading and assistance with the typing of the manuscript; and Mr G. Parry, for his photographic assistance in the preparation of this volume.

I am indebted to the following for their co-operation and assistance: Cammell Laird Archive Department; Liverpool Branch of the World Ship Society; Liverpool Maritime Museum; Imperial War Museum; and Oxton Photo Library, Birkenhead.

I am also grateful for the contributions received from Mr P. Bolger, Mr P. Welsh, Mr N. West and Mr D. Whale.

I was fortunate to add to my own collection the extensive slide collection of the late J. H. Williams, the photographic prints of the late K. W. Green, and the photographic negatives of the late G. Kissack. The three gentlemen were my lifelong friends.

BIBLIOGRAPHY

Anderson, R. and Hallam, R. B. *White Star*
Dunn, L. *Famous Liners of the Past*
Hyde, F. *Liverpool and the Mersey*
Isherwood, J. *Steamers of the Past*
Le Fleming, H. M. *Warships of World War I*
Lenton, H. T. and Colledge, J. J. *Warships of World War II*
Mersey Docks and Harbour Board *Business in Great Waters*
Miller, W. *Trans-Atlantic Liners*
Shaun, J. and Hayhart, W. *Majesty at Sea*
World Ship Society *Canadian Pacific 1891-1956*
Engineering 1904-1930
Sea Breezes

CONTENTS

INTRODUCTION

This is the story of just one of Liverpool's docks, the Gladstone, and of the liners that sailed to and from the Port of Liverpool.

Many docks in ports throughout the world can lay claim to fame for some or other particular reason, but it is doubtful whether any can match the importance or significance of Liverpool's Gladstone Dock, which throughout its history has been associated with and reflected the changing mercantile and naval fortunes of Britain.

Situated in Bootle at the northern end of the dock system, Gladstone Dock was built on land owned by the Mersey Docks & Harbour Board, and at the time of construction was regarded as the world's largest civil engineering project. Progress on the work, which was commenced in 1910, was interrupted by the outbreak of war in 1914, and, consequently, it took over 20 years to complete. When the Gladstone Dock Estate was ceremoniously opened in 1927 it also entered the record books for having the largest area of enclosed water for any dock in the world.

This dock, more than any on either side of the River Mersey, mirrored the changes in commercial fortune that affected Merseyside during the course of the 20th century, and now is an appropriate time to turn the research spotlight on this historic dock. The first decade of the present century saw Liverpool's dock facilities unable to cope with the ever-increasing volume of freight and passenger traffic. The congestion became so acute that the Mersey Docks & Harbour Board had to acknowledge the need for a substantial increase in its dock capacity.

The response, although belated, was an imaginative

Above left Gladstone Dock past and present. After it was opened in July 1913 the dock was used by various cargo steamers, but owing to problems with silt interfering with the movement of the sliding caisson, it was October before the dock could be used for its other duty - that of a graving dock. The first liner involved was the *Lusitania*, seen here preparing to undergo a hull inspection. The pumping station, consisting of a diesel plant driving centrifugal pumps, was exceedingly powerful, and was capable of draining the dock in a matter of four hours. Note the railway line on the south side of the dock, which was very necessary when the new *Aquitania* was bunkered. *D. Whale*

Left A view looking into the former graving dock today. The pumping station was to the right of the entrance; the tanks on the right are for the storage of latex rubber, while those at the far end of the dock contain edible oils. In its new role as 'No 3 Branch', the dock acts as a 'ro-ro' terminal for commercial vehicles *en route* to Northern Ireland. The vessels used are large carriers whose names, *Buffalo* and *Bison*, match their modern appearance. *G. Parry*

and prestigious project the completion of which was delayed by the 1914-18 War. However, the Gladstone graving dock, the only part of the project completed by 1914, played a vital part in Britain's war effort.

The cessation of hostilities in 1918 led to a resumption of work on the Gladstone project culminating in its official opening in 1927. Initial euphoria in the port of Liverpool was shattered by the 1929 Stock Market crash and subsequent economic depression, followed by efforts in the mid-1930s to regenerate passenger traffic by using laid-up liners for cheap holiday cruising. These developments were reflected in the performance of the Gladstone Dock during that period.

The dock's busiest and most important period was during the Second World War, 1939-45. Not only was the Battle of the Atlantic commanded from the basement Headquarters of Derby House in Liverpool, but the Gladstone's quayside and dry dock facilities were indispensable in the successful conduct of that campaign.

In the post-war period the Gladstone saw itself spearheading the drive for Britain's economic recovery, the success or failure of which depended on the efforts to recapture and, if possible, to expand overseas trade markets. For a short period passenger liners resumed their pre-eminent position in the Mersey until the steady expansion of air travel began to compete seriously with and, ultimately, to supersede sea travel. That the post-war effort did not succeed was not solely due to what happened in Britain's docks and on board British ships. It is true that these post-war years witnessed bitter and protracted industrial disputes, including several dock and seamen's strikes, but notwithstanding these the pattern of Britain's trade was changing. Liverpool is Britain's Gateway to the West and the North Atlantic, while after 1970 the nation's economic ties became increasingly strengthened with Europe.

Liverpool and Gladstone Dock found themselves on the 'wrong' side of Britain, and the late 1970s and 1980s witnessed a period of decline. This process was arrested to some extent by the construction of the Seaforth Container Terminal, with Gladstone Dock assuming a subsidiary role.

The future cannot be predicted with any degree of certainty or assurance. The opening of the Channel Tunnel might provide the Port of Liverpool with an opportunity for commercial resurgence, not as Britain's but as Europe's 'Gateway to the West'. Should that occur, it is a fair bet that the final chapter in the history of Gladstone Dock has not been written. Only time will tell.

This volume deals with the passenger side of Liverpool's involvement in that story; it is hoped that another volume will deal with the freight story. The photographs in the five chapters will evoke many memories for older readers, while the more youthful, who have only known the Gladstone in its period of decline, may be pleasantly surprised and even amazed at the revelation of its past glories.

A Chronology of Gladstone Dock

1906	Parliamentary powers are received to develop land at Bootle beyond Hornby Dock.
1910	Work commences on a new river channel to the new dock.
1913	Dual-purpose dock is opened by King George V and named Gladstone Dock.
1921	First dock is closed and work commences on the complete three-branch Estate.
1927	Completed Estate and new river entrance are opened by King George V.
1962	New Langton river entrance is opened by Queen Elizabeth II.
1967	Work commences on new Seaforth Dock.
1967	Gladstone Graving Dock closes, to become container terminal.
1972	New Royal Seaforth Estate is opened by the Princess Royal.

1. BACKGROUND TO THE NEW DOCK, 1895-1913

During the latter half of the 19th century Liverpool became Britain's No 1 port for passengers wishing to travel to America, and earned for itself the soubriquet 'The Gateway to the West'. The shipping and commerce of the Mersey were exceeded only by those of the Thames with its Port of London and also Tilbury.

Liverpool's premier position was first threatened in the 1890s after the London & South Western Railway purchased Southampton Docks in 1892 and initiated substantial improvements. Southampton Water is fortunate in enjoying a protracted high water due to the tidal flows from the Solent and also from Spithead. The new owners soon realised that the question of a quick 'turn-round' for ships was of paramount importance. Ships are very expensive and individual investments, and earn no dividends for their owners when they are idle and not at sea.

Because of the Mersey's remarkably high tides, often as much as 32 feet, the docks had to be enclosed by a wall some 10 feet thick and reaching 12 feet above the maximum high-water mark. Access to the docks was gained by three main entrances located at Canada, Sandon and Brunswick docks and connected to the river by half-tide basins. The need to use these sea locks caused delays to liners, which frequently spent hours at anchor in the river waiting for the tide in order to enter dock and, when tides were exceptionally low, even to reach the Landing Stage to discharge their passengers.

Five famous companies competed for the passenger and mail traffic to North America: Allan and Dominion running to Canada, and Cunard, White Star and the American-owned Inman & International running to the United States. The Americans in particular were dissatisfied with the delays experienced at Liverpool and were easily enticed to Southampton by the advantages offered there; care had been taken to ensure that the new Ocean docks on the Solent were open basins whose quays could be reached by the largest liners at all states of the tide, and where they were able to conduct the whole business of the turn-round between voyages without further movement.

Liverpool's docks were owned and managed by the Mersey Docks & Harbour Board, and the loss of the American liners concentrated the minds of the Board members to consider counter-measures. One proposal was to utilise a large area of land at the north end of the system and construct an estate that would provide direct access from the river at all states of the tide for even the largest ships. Some members of the Board who were mainly concerned with cargo traffic, including the Chairman, Alfred Holt, considered that the money could be better spent on improving existing facilities.

It was finally decided as a compromise to deepen the bed of the river at the Landing Stage and to widen the entrance at Sandon from 80 feet to 100 feet. These were wise decisions as they would enable the new large vessels already planned by Cunard to reach the company's berths at Huskisson Dock and the Board's largest graving dock at Canada Dock. However, these improvements would do nothing to cut the waiting time caused by the Mersey tides.

In 1902 the White Star Line joined the powerful International Mercantile Marine, which was financed by American capital, and decided to build two of the world's largest lines. To conform with American practice they would terminate their No 1 passenger and mail service from New York at Southampton. Once again the Dock Board saw passenger shipping moving away from Liverpool, and the new dock proposal was re-examined. This time it was suggested that a three-branch estate should be constructed, including a dry dock that could accommodate ships up to 1,000 feet in length. Parliamentary powers were approved in 1906, but the idea was shelved when it was estimated that the cost of the work would be over £2 million.

In 1905 Cunard Line began to build its new super-liners, which were expected to be not only the fastest in the world, but also the largest, with a length of 790 feet and a beam of 88 feet. The fear of losing these also to Southampton was allayed when Cunard declared its intention of continuing to use Liverpool as its terminal port. As it was expected that the ships would spend only five days in port before sailing again, Cunard had no wish to arrange for the new ships to enter dock unless it was specially necessary. Instead it asked that a large buoy be moored in the river off Woodside, at which the liners could complete the turn-round. This was provided, and additional measures included the removal of a further large quantity of rock and silt from the bed of the river at the Landing Stage, whose passenger facilities were further improved by the fitting of an upper deck. The two super-liners, named *Lusitania* and *Mauretania*, duly entered service and, although capable of their designed speed of

25 knots, it was usually found necessary to use a third ship in order to maintain a weekly transatlantic service. Either the much older *Campania* or the *Lucania* was used until a third super-liner could enter service.

In 1910 Cunard duly announced that it was ordering a third vessel to match the luxury of the first pair, but she would be considerably bigger to compete with the rapidly increasing size of Atlantic liners. It was expected that her tonnage would be 45,500 with a length of 901 feet and a beam of 97 feet - the thousand-foot liner had almost arrived. Cunard was certainly not prepared to service so large a ship at the river buoy, and stated that unless a dock was forthcoming that could accommodate the new *Aquitania*, the service would have to move to Southampton.

At last the Dock Board decided on a positive course of action. A modern dock estate would be built, but there would certainly not be sufficient time to complete a three-branch project before the new ship came into service. Consequently it was decided to build the new estate in two stages to ensure that there would be adequate

accommodation in time. It would be something of a race between the new ship and the new dock - fortunately the dock won by some nine months.

The first stage, which was completed by April 1913, entailed the construction of a single basin 1,050 feet in length. Its 120-foot-wide entrance was connected by a direct channel to the Mersey and was consequently capable of being used at all stages of the tide. The basin would have dual functions: when flooded, cargo could be handled using the latest quayside equipment and transport facilities, and when 'dried out' it would become the largest graving dock in the world. Originally it had been hoped that the whole estate would be finished by the summer of 1918.

King George V and Queen Mary duly opened the graving dock on 11 July 1913 and the occasion included one of the finest parades of shipping ever seen on the Mersey. The Royal Party steamed through the lines of ships aboard the Dock Board's tender *Galatea*. Unfortunately the Great War prevented any further construction work, and it was to be 14 years before the estate was completed.

In the 1890s Liverpool became known as 'The Gateway to the West' because all the principal passenger liners sailing to North and South America commenced their voyages from the Mersey. The main American line was the Inman & International Steamship Company, whose two largest vessels were the *City of Paris* and the *City of New York*, each with a gross weight of 10,000 tons and, at the time, claimed to be the largest liners in the world. The graceful lines of the *City of Paris* are apparent in **this view of the vessel at anchor in the River Mersey. They were the first of the great ships to forsake the port of Liverpool for Southampton, the Americans disliking the time that was wasted waiting in the River Mersey until the tide was sufficiently high to enable them to enter the docks. Later these two liners became part of the American Line and, as the *Paris* and *New York*, were rebuilt with just two funnels and managed to survive the 1914-18 War.**

MARITIME HERITAGE

Above The two famous companies that rivalled the Americans on the North Atlantic were the Cunard and White Star Lines, which owned some of the fastest vessels afloat. Cunard's record-breakers *Umbria* and *Etruria* competed not only with the American ships but also with White Star's *Germanic* and *Britannic* for the fastest passages from Liverpool to New York. These vessels were then superseded respectively by Cunard's *Campania* and *Lucania*, and White Star's *Teutonic* and *Majestic*. By 1894 liners had reached a gross tonnage of nearly 13,000, and the transatlantic passage had been reduced to 5⅓ days. The *Etruria* is seen here in the Mersey dressed overall to celebrate Queen Victoria's birthday in 1889.

Below As the size of liners increased, ship-owners incessantly enquired of the Mersey Docks & Harbour Board about its intentions to construct new docks, particularly at the north end of Liverpool. The most recent dock to have been built at this time was

Toxteth to the south in 1888, preceded by Hornby to the north in 1884. The Board considered the matter but the Chairman, Alfred Holt, was of the opinion that freight interests were more important than passenger liners and declared that, provided the docks could cope with vessels of 600 feet in length, 70 feet in beam and 27 feet draft, existing facilities would suffice for the next 20 or 30 years. Fortunately more far-sighted views prevailed, and the decision was taken to widen the entrance to Sandon Dock to 100 feet and to increase the area of the Canada Dock so that longer vessels could be turned into the berths at Huskisson. This work was completed in 1897 and proved to be a very wise decision.

In this view the latest liner of the White Star Line is seen turning into Huskisson No 2 Branch. *Oceanic* was one of a pair ordered from Harland & Wolff in Belfast in 1899, but her sister ship was never built. Her dimensions were 685 feet in length and 68 feet in beam; with a gross tonnage of 17,272 she was the first vessel to exceed the size of the *Great Eastern*. D. Whale

Above Another view of the *Oceanic*, this time at the floating Landing Stage preparing to embark passengers for America. Alongside her is the White Star tender *Magnetic*. Many of the passengers would have travelled from London to Riverside station, adjacent to the Landing Stage, on the boat trains run by the London & North Western Railway Company. The end gable of the station is just visible above the *Oceanic*'s bow. *D. Whale*

Right A typical Landing Stage scene with passengers embarking and relatives and friends waiting for the liner to cast off, in this case the record-breaking Cunarder *Campania*. This is an early view of the stage before the upper landing was built.

Left In 1902 the White Star Line merged with the Morgan Combine. This was a large American shipping empire officially known as the International Mercantile Marine, and, as a result, financial control of White Star passed out of British hands. The President of this Company, J. B. Ismay, had funds available to increase the size of the White Star fleet and ordered two large liners with considerable cargo-carrying capacity: the *Celtic* of 20,900 tons and the *Cedric* of 21,035 tons. These were to join the *Oceanic* on the Liverpool-New York service. The *Celtic* is seen here in 1902 passing through the Sandon entrance from the river *en route* to Huskisson No 2 Branch, the quays of which were used by the White Star liners.

Calm weather is a rare experience on Merseyside and the Landing Stage in its exposed position takes the full force of the south-westerly and north-westerly winds, which are the prevailing climatic features in this part of the British Isles. This view of the Landing Stage as it was 100 years ago bears eloquent testimony to the bleak conditions that passengers could experience. As the size of liners and, consequently, the number of passengers increased, complaints became vociferous. However, this state of affairs lasted until 1907 when moveable covered approaches to the liners were provided for protection from the weather for passengers using the new super-liners *Lusitania* and *Mauretania*. Noteworthy is the hansom cab rank on the upper roadway

and, in the background, the Albert Dock complex without the Pier Head buildings restricting the view.

The liner in the foreground is the White Star *Adriatic* of 3,888 gross tons. Built by Harland & Wolff, she carried 50 1st Class, 40 2nd Class and 800 3rd Class passengers. On 11 April 1872 the *Adriatic* commenced her maiden voyage from Liverpool to New York. For most of her life she ran on the Liverpool-New York service, and succeeded in reducing the transatlantic crossing time to 7 days 23 hours 17 minutes. She was finally broken up at Preston in 1909. The White Star tender *Magnetic* is seen approaching on the right. *Oxton Studios*

A well-known shipping company operating from Liverpool to Canada was the Dominion Line, which, like the White Star Line, later joined the Morgan Combine. In Dominion Line days the *Labrador* of 4,737 tons is seen here at the Landing Stage in 1898. The Dominion Line shared with the Allen Line the Liverpool-Glasgow-Montreal service before White Star and later Cunard became interested in the traffic. At this time the Canadian Pacific Railway Company confined its activities to cargo-passenger sailings.

Also berthed at the Stage and ahead of the *Labrador* in this view is the tug *Great Britain*, owned by the Liverpool Steam Tug Company. On 1 March 1899 the *Labrador* foundered on the Skerryvore rocks.

While running with the Combine the two largest Dominion liners were the *Canada* and the *Dominion*, both of about 9,500 tons. Another liner built for the Dominion Line was the *Columbus*, a fine vessel of 15,300 tons and seen here leaving the Mersey. Soon afterwards she was transferred to White Star and renamed *Republic*. In 1907 she collided with the Italian steamship *Florida* off the American eastern seaboard. When the liner sank only four lives were lost thanks to the early use of wireless to summon help quickly. The remarkably low casualty list greatly influenced the Board of Trade in respect of the number of lifeboats that modern ships of ever-increasing size should be required to carry. This subject became of paramount importance following the horrific loss of life in the *Titanic* disaster in 1912.

MARITIME HERITAGE

Two important companies operated a frequent service of passenger liners from the Mersey to South America. One was the Royal Mail Line, which was concerned with the eastern ports such as Rio de Janeiro and Buenos Aires, while the other was the Pacific Steam Navigation Company, using the Panama Canal to reach Valparaiso and other western ports.

The Royal Mail fleet operating from the Mersey claimed to have the world's largest refrigerated meat carriers. Each of these ships could also accommodate 1,000 passengers in three classes, yet with a tonnage of 12,000 they were smaller than the Royal Mail liners sailing from Southampton. The ships using the Mersey were the *Deseado* (seen here), *Demerara*, *Desna*, *Darro* and *Drina*. It was rare for one of them not to be seen in the port.

The Pacific Steam Navigation Company had the *Ortega*, *Oronsa*, *Oroya*, *Orbita* and *Orduna* operating out of Liverpool just before the outbreak of war in 1914. They could each accommodate 1,000 passengers, including emigrants in 3rd Class. The *Orbita* is seen here sailing downstream. At first the liners of the company had black funnels, but later they were painted buff, as seen here, following the merger with the Royal Mail Line.

In 1909 the 14,800-ton *Laurentic* (originally intended as the *Alberta* for the Dominion Line) joined her sister the *Megantic* on the White Star service between Liverpool and Canada. She became immensely popular with passengers, and in winter, when the St Lawrence river was frozen, made cruises to the Caribbean. She was requisitioned by the Canadian Government in 1917 and was later mined and sunk off Northern Ireland with a large cargo of bullion aboard; in an epic salvage operation over £4 million of this was recovered from the sea bed.

Right Congestion became even worse when the Canadian Pacific Company, besides operating a trans-Pacific service in addition to the trans-Continental railway, decided to compete on the North Atlantic route and ordered two new liners for the purpose, the *Empress of Britain* and *Empress of Ireland*. Both were 14,000-tonners built by Fairfields; they commenced their maiden voyages from Liverpool in 1906 and were capable of 19½ knots. The *Empress of Britain* is here seen at the Stage - why one of her lifeboats is slung out is a bit of a puzzle.

The companies that served Canada from the Mersey were constantly demanding that the Dock Board increase the capacity of the north docks. *P. Bolger*

Above Launched in 1903, the White Star liner *Baltic* was the first ship to be built with American capital after Ismay had been virtually given a blank cheque by the financier J. Pierpont Morgan. This 23,884-ton liner began her maiden voyage from Liverpool to New York on 29 July 1904. The Canada Graving Dock was the only one in Liverpool capable of accommodating her dimensions - length 709 feet and beam 75 feet - and that would not have been possible if the Sandon lock and basin had not been enlarged earlier.

With almost unlimited American capital, the White Star Line continued with its modernisation programme by ordering new tonnage from Harland & Wolff. The *Baltic* was followed by the *Adriatic* in 1907; she reached the record tonnage for that time of 24,500 and made her maiden voyage on 8 May 1907. To conform with American practice the *Adriatic* was transferred to sail from Southampton with the *Teutonic*, *Majestic* and *Oceanic*. This was another loss for Liverpool. The *Baltic* was a typical 'Liverpool' liner and is seen here in the Canada Graving Dock during one of her routine overhauls.

Left *Baltic* is seen here leaving the Landing Stage, the improvements to which made by the Dock Board in preparation for the arrival of the new super-liners *Lusitania* and *Mauretania* are clearly visible - the covered accommodation provided on the upper deck for passengers, improved lighting at the stage, and the moveable upper gangways providing better access for passengers to the liners berthed at the Stage. *C. Heywood*

Above Two 18,450-ton quadruple-screw liners were ordered by the Allen Line from Beardmore's on the Clyde, the *Alsatian* in 1913 and the *Calgarian* in 1914. The latter had a short life, being torpedoed in 1918, but the *Alsatian*, seen here, had a distinguished war career as the flagship of the Northern Patrol Blockading Squadron. After the Allen Line was taken over by Canadian Pacific during the war, she was renamed *Empress of France* and as such made her first voyage from Liverpool to Quebec.

After running on the Hamburg-Southampton-Quebec service she was sent back to the Clyde for conversion to oil-firing in 1924. Afterwards she left for the Far East via the Suez Canal to replace, on the trans-Pacific service, the *Empress of Australia*, which required new engines. In 1929 she returned to Liverpool via Suez and by this time was painted in a white hull livery. After a short spell of cruising the *Empress of France* was laid up on the Clyde and was eventually broken up at Dalmuir in 1934, ironically at the same yard where she had been built.

Right In 1905 the Cunard Line ordered two 20,000-ton liners, the *Caronia* and the *Carmania*, from John Brown's shipyard in Glasgow. The latter ship was equipped with turbines in order to assess the merits of this type of propulsion. If reports were favourable Cunard intended to install turbine propulsion in two more giant super-liners, which it was planned would regain the record for Atlantic passages from the Germans.

The *Caronia* is seen here steaming past the measured mile in the lower Clyde before being handed over to her new owners. Both ships were built for the Liverpool-New York service and became a familiar sight on the Mersey until the outbreak of war in 1914. Among seafarers the *Caronia* and *Carmania* were referred to as the 'Pretty Sisters'.

Right Congestion in Liverpool's docks was becoming acute as is evident in this view of the White Star berth in Huskisson No 2 Branch, with liners berthed alongside one another. The Cunard Line in its neighbouring branch at Huskisson was experiencing similar difficulties with its ships trying to gain access to the loading quays. Note the floating structure alongside the foremost liner - this is a coal elevator bunkering the ship for its next voyage.

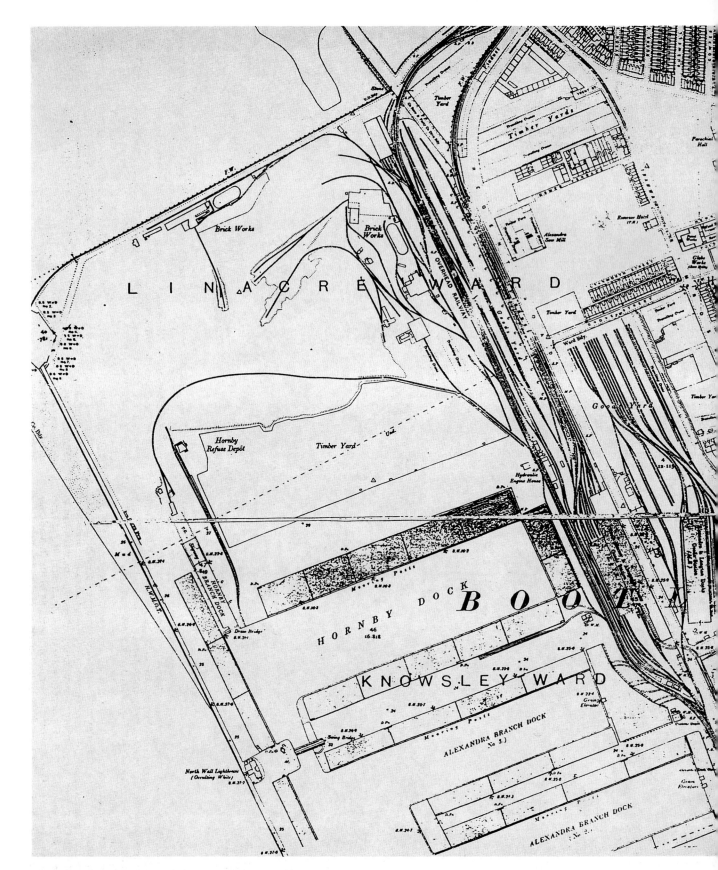

In 1906 the Mersey Docks & Harbour Board obtained Parliamentary sanction to develop land adjacent to the north of Hornby Dock, which was already in the ownership of the Board. However, when the estimated cost of the projected new dock was declared to be £2 million the Board deferred further action, but instead reached an acceptable compromise with Cunard by providing a mooring buoy in the river, dredging the approach to the Landing Stage and improving passenger facilities on the Landing Stage. This map shows the area that would have been developed.

The Cunard Line was most anxious to recapture its lost laurels from the Germans, who by now claimed to have the finest and fastest ships sailing out of New York. Cunard obtained financial assistance from the British Government to place orders for two liners, which the company hoped would achieve its objective. The *Lusitania* was ordered from John Brown's shipyard in Glasgow and the *Mauretania* from Swan Hunter of Wallsend-on-Tyne. These 32,000-tonners, with an overall length of 790 feet, would obviously tax the resources of Liverpool if Cunard continued to use the Mersey as its main terminal.

There were also special conditions that had to be met before Government assistance was provided. The ships had to be capable of maintaining a speed of 25 knots and the hulls had to satisfy Admiralty specifications with a far more elaborate subdivision of the hull than was generally found in merchant ships. The bunkers had to be arranged 'cruiser fashion', that is independently down each side of the hull. Moreover, in the event of a state of national emergency the whole of the Cunard passenger fleet had to be available for requisition by the Government at short notice.

As Cunard needed to operate the two ships on a weekly service there would not be sufficient time for them to enter dock between voyages, particularly in respect of bunkering requirements, as it was estimated that nearly 5,000 tons of coal was consumed in each ship's boilers during a transatlantic crossing. The Dock Board offered to place a large buoy in the Mersey off Woodside where the liners could make their 'turn-round', only entering dock when circumstances required them to do so. At the Landing Stage further improvements would be made by the provision of an upper deck and the deepening of the river bed so that the large ships could moor alongside at all states of the tide. Cunard was satisfied with these arrangements and, after extensive trials, *Lusitania* arrived in the Mersey for her maiden voyage, which began on 7 September 1907.

The coal elevator shown in the previous photograph depicting congestion in the Huskisson Dock was not suitable for coaling the *Lusitania* and *Mauretania* because they had no cross bunkers. Consequently it was necessary to have access to both sides when loading coal, and the most convenient location for doing this was when they were berthed at the buoy, as seen here. *P. Welsh*

Above After coaling at the buoy the *Lusitania* has now moved to the Landing Stage and awaits the arrival of the boat specials at Riverside station before sailing in the late afternoon for New York. Note the Liver Building in the course of construction and the Cunard Company's tender *Skirmisher* drawing alongside the liner. Ferry boat passengers would have found this to be a typical Saturday scene at the Liverpool Landing Stage in 1910. *Oxton Studios*

Below This picture of the *Lusitania* manoeuvring in the Sandon Basin is a good example of the difficulties involved when it was necessary to turn one of these enormous ships to reach either the Cunard berth in Huskisson Dock or the dry dock at the Canada Dock.

Right In Canada Dock, fresh from her trials, the *Lusitania* prepares for her maiden voyage. Unfortunately the bows were repainted black and the upper white portion only existed during her trials.

Below Just over one month later the *Mauretania* arrived, and this rare view shows the two new liners together in the Mersey, the *Mauretania* on the left. She left on her maiden voyage on 16 November 1907 and both ships soon regained for Britain the record for Atlantic crossings - none dare say which was the faster ship! They sailed to New York with only one intermediate call at Queenstown in Southern Ireland, but it soon became apparent that a weekly schedule could not be maintained from Liverpool with just two liners, even if they were able to achieve 26 knots. Depending on availability, either the *Lucania* or the *Campania* was used to fill the gap, but neither of these old ships could match the luxury and comfort of the new ships.

Cunard informed the Dock Board that, as soon as finance allowed, it would order another liner from John Brown's shipyard on the Clyde, to match the standards set by the *Lusitania* and *Mauretania*. Cunard's rivals, the White Star Line, had already announced its plans for a new three-ship service from Southampton and, to keep pace with the continual increase in the size of passenger ships, they would be between 45,000 and 48,000 tons. Accordingly Cunard decided that its third ship, to be named *Aquitania*, would be of 45,650 tons, 901 feet in

length and with a beam of 97 feet. The new super-liner was due to be in service in 1914.

The *Mauretania* had already broken away from the buoy in the Mersey during a winter storm, but fortunately she was re-moored without sustaining any damage. Cunard announced that it was not prepared to turn the *Aquitania* round in mid-river, and that if a new dock of suitable proportions was not made available, the service would be transferred to Southampton.

Above As the *Mauretania* prepares to leave the Landing Stage at the commencement of another transatlantic voyage, large liners can be seen in the Mersey waiting for the tide in order to enter to dock. It was this time-wasting factor that did much to persuade shipping companies owning expensive liners to forsake the Mersey in favour of the Solent.

Below On 14 June 1911 the *Olympic*, the first of the new White Star liners, sailed up the Mersey on a combined courtesy and publicity visit, and for the first time Liverpudlians saw a liner that could not get into the port's docks. She was, however, thrown open to the public and thousands took the opportunity to examine the liner's sumptuous appointments; the proceeds were donated to the Seamen's Mission and associated charities. It was also intended to arrange a similar publicity call for White Star's second liner, the *Titanic*, but delays caused by a coal strike led to cancellation of the visit and she went straight from Belfast to Southampton from where she commenced her fateful maiden voyage. As a result the *Titanic* never visited the port whose registration name she displayed on her stern.

The visit by the *Olympic* to the port of Liverpool and Cunard's demands regarding the *Aquitania* impressed upon the Dock Board the urgent need to concentrate all its resources on the construction of the new Gladstone Graving Dock. Fortunately the Board had already obtained Parliamentary sanction in 1906 to build a three-branch dock estate on land they owned at Seaforth in Bootle, but there plainly would not be sufficient time to complete the whole project before the *Aquitania* arrived. It was decided, therefore, to construct the new estate in two stages. The first stage would consist of just one basin, which could be used either as a wet dock for cargo handling or as a dry dock for ship repairs. The dock would be 1,050 feet long with an entrance 120 feet wide. It would be connected directly with the river by a channel adequately protected from silting and erosion by substantial walls and embankments.

THE NEW GLADSTONE DOCKS, LIVERPOOL.

Above The Gladstone project attracted the attention of postcard manufacturers. This one, depicting an artist's fanciful impression of the proposed development, is undated, but must be pre-1921 because the Tower at New Brighton, which is a prominent feature in the background, was demolished in 1919-21; it was higher than that at Blackpool! The artist had obviously not seen the plan and elevation of the dock sheds, while the uncluttered open spaces indicate that he had never been anywhere near a dock in his life!

However, the claim that Gladstone Dock would be 'the largest in the world' was correct at the time. *C. Heywood*

Below The reality in a similar photographic view of work on the graving dock well under way. Seen from an overhead train, in the foreground sightseers are either looking over the wall or peering through the fence to check on the progress being made. Thus it ever was and always will be. *Mersey Docks & Harbour Board.*

GLADSTONE DOCK LIVERPOOL
LARGEST GRAVING DOCK IN THE WORLD
(IN COURSE OF COMPLETION)
VIEW FROM THE OVERHEAD RAILWAY AT SEAFORTH SANDS

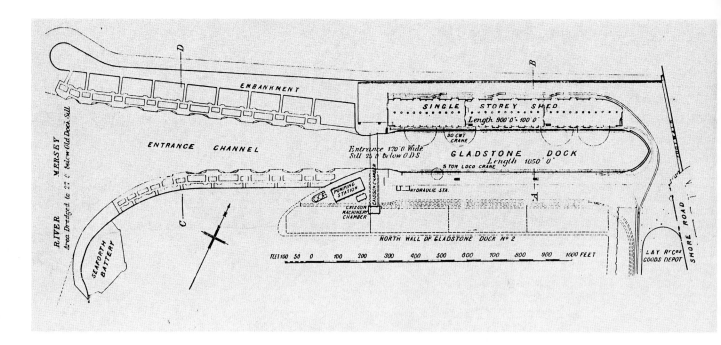

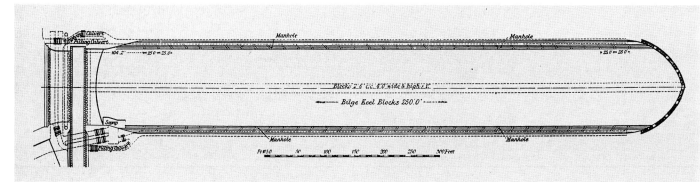

Top A general plan of the Gladstone Graving Dock. The Entrance Channel was 1,200 feet long and 400 feet wide at the river end, tapering to the 120-foot-wide Dock Entrance. *Mersey Docks & Harbour Board*

Above A larger-scale plan of the dock itself. *Mersey Docks & Harbour Board*

Right A plan of the dock showing the location of the pumping station and caisson chamber. The prominent cooling tower for the diesel engines is also shown. The 124-foot-long caisson was manufactured by the Motherwell Bridge Company and was of the sliding rather than floating type. If the latter had been adopted, two caissons would have been required, one for keeping water in the dock when the tide was lower then the water level in the dock, and the other for keeping the tidal water out when the dock was emptied. The caisson slid along greenheart sills and over polished granite blocks. The pumping station could empty the dock of its 44,000,000 gallons of water in 4 hours. *Mersey Docks & Harbour Board*

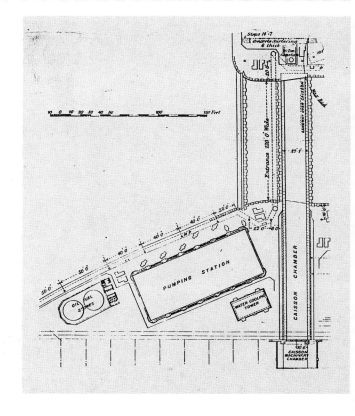

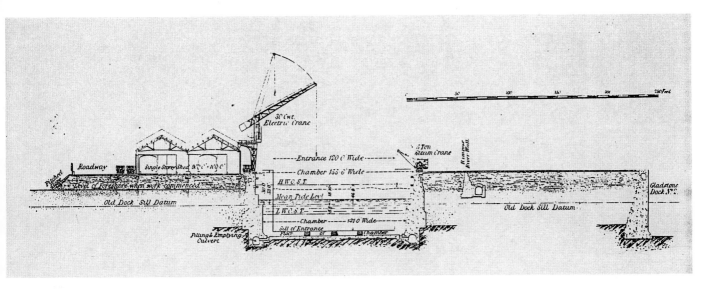

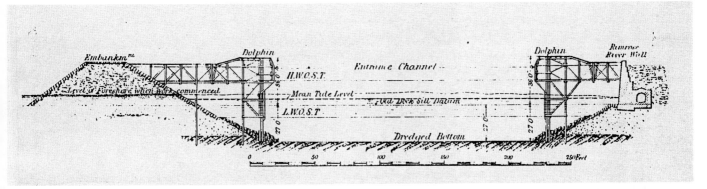

Top A section through the dock along the line A-B on the plan opposite. *Mersey Docks & Harbour Board*

Above A section through the Entrance Channel along the line C-D on the plan opposite. *Mersey Docks & Harbour Board*

Looking down the Graving Dock towards Seaforth and Litherland; the navvies are dwarfed by their surroundings. To construct the graving dock steam excavators removed 165,000 cubic yards of clay and 64,000 cubic yards of sandstone rock. *Mersey Docks & Harbour Board*

The size of the contractors' railway wagons visible on different levels gives some idea of the immense scale of the engineering works. This is part of the Long Channel retaining wall located at 'C' on the general plan on page 24. *Mersey Docks & Harbour Board*

The dock nearing completion. Note the single-storey shed on the north side, which was 900 feet long and 100 feet wide. Massive wooden 'dolphins' were erected with heavy supports to the embankment to cut down silting and erosion, and were also similarly placed on the south side of the channel with supports from the concrete wall. Note the culvert contained within the wall for the diverted Rimrose Brook; the outfall from the pumping station when the dock was being drained was also directed into this culvert. Compared with building costs today, it is difficult to believe that the Gladstone Graving Dock project cost £500,000 and was planned and carried out by the Engineering Department of the Mersey Docks & Harbour Board, under the direction of the Board's Engineer in Chief, Mr A. G. Lyster. *Mersey Docks & Harbour Board*

The completed dock ready for opening, July 1913. The Mersey Docks & Harbour Board took every opportunity to publicise its prestigious project, and commissioned the production of excellent quality picture postcards, which were used in official correspondence. The two figures seen in the bottom of the graving dock in this postcard view give a good indication of its colossal scale. The recipients of such a communication cannot fail to have been impressed with the Board's enterprise and initiative. *C. Heywood*

MARITIME HERITAGE

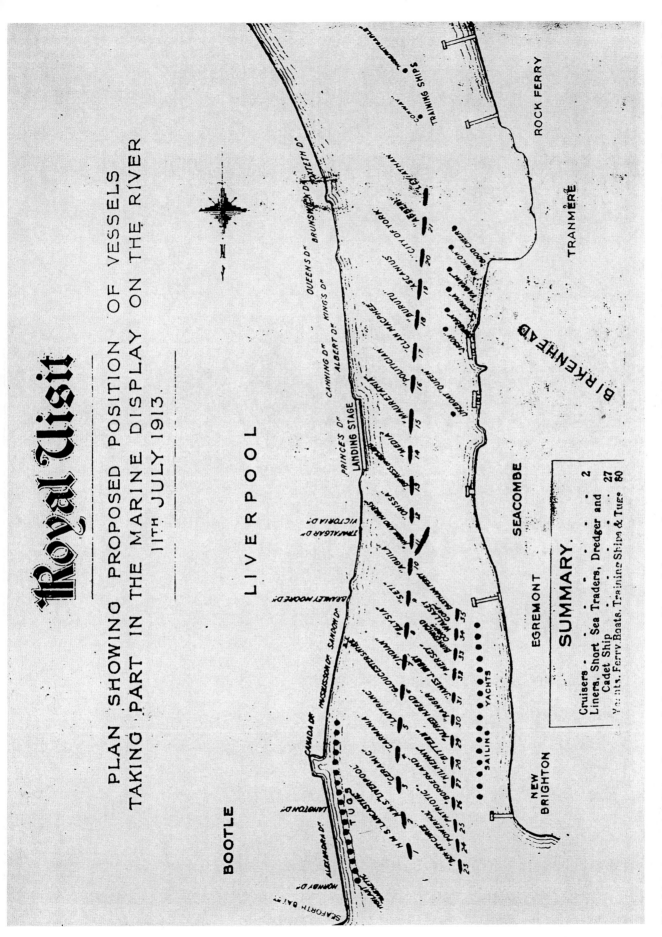

Royal Visit

PLAN SHOWING PROPOSED POSITION OF VESSELS TAKING PART IN THE MARINE DISPLAY ON THE RIVER

11TH JULY 1913.

BOOTLE

LIVERPOOL

ROCK FERRY

TRANMERE

BIRKENHEAD

SEACOMBE

EGREMONT

NEW BRIGHTON

TRAINING SHIPS

SUMMARY.

Cruisers - - - -	2
Liners, Short Sea Traders, Dredger and Cadet Ship - -	27
Yachts, Ferry Boats, Training Ships & Tugs	80

It had become a race between the new dock and the new ship, and, fortunately, the dock won by some nine months. It was opened by King George V and Queen Mary on 11 July 1913, to be named the Gladstone Dock. Drawn up in the River was a great pageant of ships of all sizes including many well-known Liverpool ships and headed by two cruisers, HMS *Liverpool* and HMS *Lancaster*.

Above The cavalcade of ships in the river proved to be a popular attraction; the Wallasey ferry boat is doing a roaring trade, as is the owner of the rowing-boat! The three ships in mid-river reading from the left are the *Empress of Ireland*, *Media* and *Mauretania*.

Below The Royal Party boarded the *Galatea* at the Landing Stage, then sailed through the lines of merchant ships. The *Galatea* is here passing the Harrison liner *Politician*, and beyond lies the *Mauretania*, which was then the world's fastest liner and which the Royal Party called to inspect before continuing to Gladstone Dock.

MARITIME HERITAGE

Above This extract details the music played and the timetable arranged for the Royal opening proceedings. *C. Heywood*

Right The *Galatea* called at the Seaforth Battery, where the King inspected the Guard of Honour. In the background is the Cunard liner *Caronia*. *Mersey Docks & Harbour Board*

Galatea at the head of the dock, showing some of the ornate stands erected for guest spectators. The dock was named 'Gladstone' after the recently retired Chairman of the Dock Board, Robert Gladstone. After the ceremony the Royal Party proceeded to Bootle, Oriel Road, station, where the Royal Train was waiting to take them back to London. *Mersey Docks & Harbour Board*

LIVERPOOL AND THE MERSEY

Left After it was opened the dock was used by various cargo steamers - the first being Moss Line's *Memphis*, which discharged a load of cotton into the shed. Owing to problems with silt interfering with the movement of the sliding caisson, it was October 1913 before the dock could be used for its other duty, that of a graving dock.

Cunard applied to gain exclusive use of Gladstone Dock for its three large express liners, but this was declined by the Board, one of the reasons for the dock's construction being to ease the overall congestion at the North Docks. Only the *Aquitania* had the guaranteed use of the dock between voyages, and the *Lusitania* and *Mauretania* continued to be turned round at the buoy.

The dock was used by various vessels until the *Aquitania* arrived from her trials on 14 May 1914. It was a misty day and she is seen here coming down the long channel on her way to the graving dock in order to get her final coat of paint.

Below Viewed from a train on the Liverpool Overhead Railway, the *Aquitania* has had her final coat of paint and last-minute checks prior to her move to the Landing Stage to embark passengers for her maiden voyage.

The *Aquitania* is berthed at the Landing Stage waiting to commence her maiden voyage to New York on 30 May 1914. This should have been a day of great jubilation, but unfortunately the day before news had reached Liverpool of the sinking of the *Empress of Ireland* following a collision with the Norwegian collier *Storstad* in the St Lawrence River. The loss of life had been catastrophic - 840 passengers and 172 crew, most of the latter being Liverpool men.

There was nothing revolutionary in the *Aquitania*'s design apart from her imposing exterior appearance. Internally she was magnificent. Nothing had been spared by

Cunard and she soon earned the soubriquet 'Ship beautiful' among seafarers. Ahead of the *Aquitania* and adding to the waterfront pollution is the Isle of Man ferry *Tynwald* about to leave with another full load of holidaymakers, mainly from the North of England.

With the *Lusitania*, *Mauretania* and *Aquitania* sailing regularly each Saturday direct to New York, Liverpool and also the Cunard Line could boast of having the finest service between the United Kingdom and the United States of America. It was, alas, to be very short-lived, because war clouds were rapidly gathering on the horizon.

2. THE FIRST WORLD WAR 1914-18

The first Gladstone Dock played an enormous part in assisting the country's war effort in the dark days of 1914-18, but many details of its activities have never been revealed for security reasons. However, the log of the pumping station has been preserved and from it can be obtained the names of many of the ships for which it was prepared as

The *Aquitania* only completed three round voyages and was in Liverpool preparing for her next one when it was considered that war was so near that the Government exercised their lien on the Cunard passenger fleet by selecting her for conversion into an Armed Merchant Cruiser (AMC) to sail under the White Ensign.

The Palladian Lounge of the *Aquitania* had been decorated in the style of George I and was one of the most sumptuous ever to be fitted in an ocean liner. The ceiling centre piece was an 18th-century painting, which had been removed from a Dutch house of the period and fitted in the lounge. Other public rooms were just as lavishly decorated in styles ranging from Charles II and Christopher Wren to Louis XVI.

The furniture and fittings were removed from the liner in the incredible time of four days and were stored in Gladstone's north quayside shed, which had been requisitioned by the Admiralty on the outbreak of war. After the war everything was put back on board, but the job then took much more than four days!

a graving dock, as seen in the accompanying table. From other sources it is possible to identify the military purpose for using the dry dock by many of the vessels named.

When hostilities commenced on 4 August 1914 all the sailings of passenger liners from the Mersey were cancelled. It was generally believed that there were many marauding German cruisers at large in the world's oceans and owners were reluctant to risk losing their expensive ships. It became extremely difficult for ordinary people to obtain passages overseas as most of the liners, including the *Aquitania*, were requisitioned on the outbreak of war either for trooping or for conversion into AMCs (Armed Merchant Cruisers). Of the remaining Cunard pair, the *Mauretania,* which was homeward-bound, was diverted to Halifax in Canada and eventually returned to Liverpool on 14 August, while the *Lusitania,* which was in New

York, finally made a transatlantic dash for home. She made it, but only after being pursued by the German cruiser *Dresden.* Only her superior speed saved her.

Because there were now no French or German liners crossing the Atlantic there was an enormous build-up of civilians trying to obtain passages to the United States or to Canada, and consequently emergency arrangements had to be made to find them berths; both the *Lusitania* and *Mauretania* made four round voyages at high speed to rescue stranded Americans. However, the enormous appetite for fuel resulting from the average speed of 24 knots was unacceptable. Subsequently a weekly schedule between Liverpool and New York was authorised by the Government to be operated by Cunard on a non-profit-making basis. The service would be provided by the *Lusitania* (restricted to 19 knots), the new PSNC *Orduna*

Extract from the log of the Pumping Station at Gladstone Graving Dock, 1913-1921

1913	11 July		Dock officially opened.
	Oct	*Lusitania*	First ship to use it as a graving dock.
1914	May	*Aquitania*	New from trials.
	Aug	*Aquitania*	Conversion to Armed Merchant Cruiser (AMC).
		HMS *Erin*	New from Vickers for modification.
	Sept	*Aquitania*	Repairs after collision with *Canadian*.
	Oct-Spring of 1915		Dock cleared for 'Jobs' - Admiralty code for work on converting liners to AMCs or 'dummy' battleships.
1915	May	*Mauretania*	Conversion to troopship.
		Aquitania	Conversion to troopship.
	Oct	HMS *Barham*	New from John Brown's on completion of trials.
		Olympic	Conversion to troopship.
	Nov	*Cedric*	Conversion to troopship (from AMC with 10th Cruiser Sqn).
		Britannic	From Harland's to commission as hospital ship.
1916	Jan	HMS *St Vincent*	Operational refit.
		Aquitania	Conversion to hospital ship.
		HMS *Revenge*	New from Vickers on completion of trials.
	May	*Olympic*	Conversion to troopship and 'dazzle' painting.
		Celtic	From 10th Cruiser Sqn - conversion to troopship.
		Cedric	For refit.
1917	Feb	*Celtic*	Mined off Mersey Bar - in for repairs.
	Apr	*Lapland*	Mined off Mersey Bar - in for repairs.
	May	*Justicia*	Intended as *Statendam* - requisitioned new as a troopship under White Star management.
	Sept	HMS *Ramillies*	New from Beardmore's - damaged on launch.
	Nov	*Leviathan*	US troopship - for dazzle painting.
1918	Jan	*Cedric*	Repairs after collision with *Montreal*.
	Apr	*Aquitania*	Armed for transport of US troops.
	July	*Mauretania*	Armed for transport of US troops.
	Dec	*Aquitania*	Repairs after ramming USS *Shaw*.
1919	Feb	*Olympic*	De-requisitioned - thence to Belfast.
		Imperator	War Reparations Vessel - for refit.
	May	*Aquitania*	Returned to Cunard - fittings replaced from store.
1920	Jun	*Aquitania*	Hull repainting.
		Olympic	Hull repainting.
1921	Feb	*Imperator*	Moved to Southampton for completion of refit.

Dock closed for completion of Gladstone Estate.

Mersey Docks & Harbour Board

and two Anchor Line ships, the *Caledonia* and *California*, both of which were later torpedoed in 1917. The *Lusitania* often flew the Stars and Stripes when she had a large complement of Americans in order to deter attack by German submarines.

The Government did not commandeer all passenger liners in 1914, but those remaining could not be used as their owners wished. Voyages were not scheduled but occurred as circumstances both demanded and permitted, being dependent on the authorisation of the Board of Trade after consideration of naval intelligence reports. The ships concerned were a motley assortment of mainly the older vessels in company fleets. Cunard ran the *Caronia*, *Laconia* and *Franconia* to New York. The White Star liners *Megantic*, *Laurentic*, *Cretic* and *Canopic* sailed to Canada, as did the Allen liners *Corsican* and *Corinthian*, together with the Dominion liners *Canada* and *Dominion*.

Left and below Prewar and wartime views of the *Caronia*, one of the Cunard liners that was not requisitioned by the Government in 1914. Like all other vessels still under company control she sailed, when permitted, on her own and not in convoy. Such vessels relied on their speed to keep them out of trouble.

Below This is an official wartime photograph of the *Mauretania* returning from one of her famous transatlantic dashes taking stranded American passengers back home after the outbreak of war in 1914. The *Mauretania* then went to Chatham to be converted into an AMC. However, the Lords of the Admiralty soon changed their minds when they considered what had happened to the *Aquitania*, which had rapidly been converted into an AMC on the outbreak of war. She had sailed from Liverpool to reach her patrol area in the South West Approaches, and on 24 August, when she was off the Head of Kinsale (SE Ireland), she had collided with the Leyland Company's liner *Canadian*. By the 28th the *Aquitania* was back in the Mersey waiting to re-enter Gladstone Dock for repairs to her bow. Huge ocean liners were totally unsuited for deployment as AMCs, so the Admiralty decided that they should be paid off and laid up on the Clyde until a more appropriate and effective military role could be found for them.

Right After the *Aquitania* vacated Gladstone Dock a veil of secrecy descended on the activities of the graving dock, and the Pumping Station records describe the ships for which the dock had to be prepared simply as 'Job Numbers'. It is safe to assume that many of these 'jobs' were passenger liner conversions to AMCs and contraband examination vessels in order to relieve the small 'Edgar' Class cruisers, which were having a very rough time in the stormy seas of the North Atlantic.

When the flagship of the 10th Cruiser Squadron, the White Star liner *Oceanic*, was wrecked on the Island of Foula in the Shetlands on 8 September 1914, the Allen liner *Alsatian* was chosen to replace her, and she would most certainly have been one of the 'jobs'. She is seen here in the Mersey in her wartime garb before taking up her new duties as the flagship of the Squadron.

Below It did not take the Government long to find employment for the great Cunarders laid up on the Clyde. They were ideal in supporting the Dardanelles Campaign with its insatiable demand for large numbers of troop reinforcements following the disastrous Gallipoli landing, and both the *Aquitania* and *Mauretania* returned

to the Gladstone for conversion to troop ships. The *Mauretania* is seen here as a troop transport, still unarmed but with black funnels. On one trip through the Aegean a torpedo narrowly missed her.

When the *Aquitania* came out of the Gladstone, she became stuck in the Mersey mud and had to put back for examination. The *Empress of Britain* was then made ready for sailing. The movement of troops had to be re-arranged and, had this delay not occurred, then Britain's worst railway disaster at Quintinshill on 22 May 1915 would not have taken place. A troop train *en route* to Riverside station was involved in a collision in which an estimated 217 people lost their lives, most of whom were soldiers.

Below Because of the war Liverpool now began to see more of the Royal Navy - it had been rare for warships to visit the Mersey except on special occasions or when newly completed by Cammell Laird's shipyard in Birkenhead.

In October 1915 Britain's 'Super Dreadnought', HMS *Barham*, which at one time had been under construction in the same basin as the *Aquitania* in John Brown's shipyard, was ready for war service. After completing her trials she came into Gladstone Dock for

a final examination. With a length of 640 feet and a 90 1/2 feet beam and mounting eight 15-inch guns, the *Barham* presented a formidable aspect. The 'Super Dreadnoughts' were the first large naval ships to burn oil as well as coal. In the First World War HMS *Barham* was assigned to the Home Fleet based at Scapa Flow in the Orkneys, and took part in the Battle of Jutland in 1916. She survived the war unscathed.

At the end of October 1915 the *Olympic* arrived at the Gladstone for conversion to trooping. When she left the dock over 15 tons of spilt coal had to be cleared from the dock floor before another vessel could enter. The Mersey Docks & Harbour Board sent the bill for the clearance work to the Admiralty whose response is, unfortunately, unrecorded.

The *Cedric* was found to be too large and slow for service either as an AMC or as a contraband examination vessel, so she returned to the Gladstone in order to be fitted out as a troopship. She is seen here with soldiers lining her rails. The sight of all the lifeboats slung out over the side ready for lowering must have had a sobering effect on all those on board. Should the ship strike a mine or be struck by a torpedo, there was then a distinct possibility if not probability of the situation becoming a case of 'every man for himself' once the order to abandon ship had been given.

Many volunteers were brought from Canada to the Mersey in liners such as the *Megantic*, *Laurentic* and *Missenabie*. The latter was hastily completed by Barclay Curle of Glasgow as war approached. She just managed to complete her maiden voyage before the war commenced, and was one of the last ships to be sunk by a U-boat.

The Canadian Government was also operating a ship that had been built for the Egyptians - the *Heliopolis* of 11,000 tons. She was renamed *Royal George* and sailed regularly between Canada and the Mersey. After the war the Cunard Line chartered her while the *Aquitania* and *Mauretania* were being converted to oil fuel. The *Royal George* is seen here in Cunard colours. Her crew nicknamed her 'Rolling George' on account of her sailing characteristics.

MARITIME HERITAGE

The last liner ordered from Harland & Wolff by J. B. Ismay before he resigned from the IMM in 1913 was the 18,495-ton *Ceramic*. She was built for the Australian trade and ran via the Cape in both peace and war, finally being taken over by the Shaw Savill Line after an extensive refit in 1936.

Fighting a war beyond our shores necessitated the provision of hospital ships to bring home the sick and wounded, many of whom were landed at the Stage at Liverpool, then transported in hospital trains from Riverside station to military hospitals located in various parts of the country. A regular visitor to the Mersey was the *Essiquibo*, a converted Royal Mail Liner of 8,500 tons built at Harland & Wolff's Belfast yard in 1914. Here she is in conventional hospital ship rig entering Valletta Harbour, Malta, while on passage from the Dardanelles back to Liverpool.

As 1915 wore on, enormous casualties built up in the hospitals in the eastern Mediterranean, together with considerable disability among the troops due to disease. To cope with this ever-increasing number of casualties larger hospital ships were required, and both the *Aquitania* and *Mauretania* were refitted as such. The *Mauretania* was converted at Southampton, and later her Promenade Deck was glassed in to provide weather protection to injured troops who had to be accommodated on deck. The Germans made claims that infringements of the Geneva Convention were occurring and that certain hospital ships were carrying ordinary fit soldiers. They said that such vessels were travelling at night with their deck lights out and red crosses not illuminated. They branded such liners as 'black carriers' and said that they could not guarantee their safe passage. The principal coaling port in the Mediterranean was Naples where inspections were made by Swiss representatives of Red Cross, who were satisfied that the *Mauretania* was fulfilling all the Convention requirements.

Below As a result of the *Titanic* disaster the last of Ismay's trio of ships had to be extensively modified, and this delayed her maiden voyage. Originally to have been named *Gigantic*, her name was hastily changed to *Britannic,* and at the outbreak of war she lay in Harland & Wolff's yard with many of her appointments fitted, but further work stopped in preference to more urgent war construction. Although both the *Mauretania* and *Aquitania* had been converted to hospital ships, it was still not enough, so it was decided to complete the *Britannic* as a hospital ship. She was the largest ship to be launched from a British yard until the advent of the *Queen Mary*.

She left Belfast for Gladstone Dock where she was commissioned in December 1915, sailing to take up her duties after her one and only visit to Liverpool. Her appearance was somewhat marred by five enormous Topliss gantry davits for extra lifeboats (there should have been eight), but with her white hull, blue riband and two very large red crosses on each side she looked magnificent - the largest hospital ship ever!

After two trips to Mudros in the Aegean the *Britannic* was sent back to Belfast to be returned to her owners for trooping. However, the Government again requisitioned her as a hospital ship and she was back at Southampton for three more voyages. Outward bound on her sixth trip, with only crew members on board, she struck a mine believed to have been laid by a U-boat in the Kea Channel off Greece and sank in 20 minutes after another violent explosion caused either by her boilers blowing up or by coal dust igniting. Twenty lives were lost. Thus on 21 November 1916 the largest passenger liner ever to be sunk either in peace or war lay on the sea bed in one piece, but with a massive hole in her bow section.

Below The vagaries of war can lead to stark contrasts. As the *Britannic*, the world's largest hospital ship, left Gladstone Dock, her place was taken by a vessel whose purpose was to dole out death and destruction on a massive scale. In January 1916 it was the turn of HMS *St Vincent* to occupy the Gladstone for a refit. She was a standard ten-12-inch-gun Dreadnought of the Grand Fleet based at Scapa Flow. *Imperial War Museum*

MARITIME HERITAGE

Above The *Olympic* is here seen in a coat of the new 'dazzle' paint, which had been applied while she was in the Gladstone. After the evacuation from Gallipoli the large liners reverted to their role as troop carriers, camouflaged in a variety of 'dazzle' designs.

Below The effectiveness of the 'dazzle' camouflage is well demonstrated in this view of an unidentified transatlantic liner. Nevertheless, the captains of such vessels preferred to place more reliance on their superior speed to get themselves out of trouble.

Even in 1917 troops were still being sent overseas from Liverpool. Seen here loading for Salonika is the *Cretic* of 13,500 tons. She was built in 1902 as the *Hanoverian* for Frederick Leyland & Co to run between Liverpool and Boston, and was moved into the White Star fleet a year later. She was later returned to Leylands and renamed *Devonian*. After been laid up she was scrapped at Bo'ness in 1929.

MARITIME HERITAGE

Above By 1917 the carnage caused by Germany's U-boat campaign had decimated Britain's merchant fleets and the Government was becoming very concerned about the shortage of troopships. In British shipyards, and particularly at Belfast, there were several orders lying incomplete and these were hastily finished off in a 'Utility' style for war work. Among them were the *Orca* (Royal Mail), *Regina* (Dominion), *Belgenland* (Red Star) and *Vedic* (White Star). One of the largest, seen here, was the 32,234-tons *Statendam*, under construction for the Holland-America Line at the outbreak of war.

It was intended that Cunard should man her, so she was renamed *Justicia*, thereby maintaining the Cunard tradition of naming their vessels with an 'ia' ending. However, enough Cunard Company officers could not be found to man her, so she sailed under the White Star flag, although she was not renamed to conform with the 'ic' ending of White Star ships' names. She was completed as a troop transport and painted grey. After hull examination in Gladstone Dock, she made several transatlantic crossings, but sank on 19 July 1918 after being hit by no fewer than five torpedoes.

Below The Red Star *Belgenland* was another wartime 'Utility' conversion. She was placed under White Star management for the duration of the war and renamed, appropriately, *Belgic*. She is shown here in her wartime guise, and her distinctive lines made her readily identifiable whenever she sailed up the Mersey. After the war she was returned to her builders and finished as originally planned. Her wartime guise bore no resemblance to the post-war three-funnelled Red Star liner *Belgenland* (27,132 tons) sailing between Antwerp and New York.

Above During the war the *Lapland* became a familiar sight in the Mersey. Though built for the Red Star Line, a constituent of the IMM, she ran for White Star. In April 1917 she was mined off the Bar, but managed to limp home and was repaired in the Gladstone Graving Dock during the same month. After the war she was transferred to the Red Star Line and remained in service until 1933, when she was sold to Japanese shipbreakers.

Below In September 1917 HMS *Ramillies* arrived at Gladstone Dock for attention after a hazardous trip down the Irish Sea from her builders, Beardmore's on the Clyde. When she was launched her stern post was damaged, which severely affected her steering. The move to the Mersey was made in great secrecy and she was escorted by no fewer than 12 destroyers. While in the graving dock huge screens were placed around her stern to conceal the repair work. On completion of the work the *Ramillies* was experimentally camouflaged in a coat of pink paint - one can only guess at the matelots' response to this development. The experiment did not last long and standard' dazzle' paint was applied to camouflage her. When she left the Gladstone she proceeded to Scapa to add her strength to the rest of the Grand Fleet. *Imperial War Museum*

Above By 1917 most liners were adorned in the new camouflage paintwork, which, it was hoped, would make them more difficult targets for U-boats. In April of that year America declared war on Germany, and by the summer of 1918 over 2,000,000 soldiers had been shipped across the Atlantic to fight on the Western Front, many of them disembarking *en route* at Liverpool to be temporarily housed in their main transit camp at Knotty Ash on the outskirts of the city. A typical transport was the *Orduna* shown here arriving in the Mersey. *Imperial War Museum*

Below In order to get the 'Yanks' over here as soon as possible the Government decided to ignore the very extravagant fuel consumptions of the *Aquitania* and *Mauretania* and restore them to active service as troop transports after giving them a 'dazzle' paint finish. Their mission was to cross the Atlantic unescorted and to ferry US troops, usually to Liverpool. This view of the *Aquitania* in the Hudson River shows that she was still unarmed, but in the early summer of 1918 both liners went into the Gladstone to be fitted with defensive armaments.

Above When the United States entered the war many of the foreign liners that had been interned there were commandeered for war use. They included the world's largest liner, the *Vaterland* (54,300 tons). Repaired after sustaining considerable sabotage damage while in New York, she was renamed *Leviathan* and made ready for an Atlantic crossing with US troops. After a nightmare voyage she entered the Gladstone in November 1917, the largest liner ever to do so. In the Gladstone she was 'dazzle' painted, then made two more voyages to the Mersey, but after she struck the bed of the river on her third visit, the Americans subsequently rerouted her to Brest. She is seen here on her first visit to the Mersey prior to the application of the 'dazzle' camouflage. Her protective armament is clearly visible on her fore-deck.

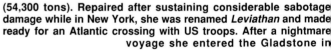

Left Another ex-German liner, the *Amerika,* was seized and put to use as the *America*, engaged on trooping duties. She is seen here waiting her turn to berth at the Landing Stage to disembark her 'doughboys'. Afterwards she would enter Gladstone Dock to make ready for her next Atlantic crossing. Noteworthy are the 'Spotting Tops' on her fore and aft masts.

Above In January 1918 the *Cedric* collided with and sank the 7,000-ton Canadian Pacific liner *Montreal*, built in 1899. The *Cedric* managed to get back to Liverpool and went into the Gladstone for repairs.

Below Both the *Aquitania* and *Mauretania* continued to sail across the Atlantic unescorted except for the last leg of the eastbound voyage through the Western Approaches, the danger area off Ireland. They were now armed, as can clearly be seen in this view of the *Mauretania* disembarking troops at the Landing Stage. Her guns were fitted while she was in the Gladstone during July 1918.

3. COMPLETION OF GLADSTONE DOCK AND THE INTER-WAR YEARS, 1919-39

The completion of new passenger tonnage had been disrupted by the war and partly built ships could be seen in most British shipyards. These, together with new orders, were soon given priority. Moreover, under the terms of the Peace Treaty, Germany forfeited her merchant fleet, and many of its vessels were purchased from the Shipping Controller to be sailed by British owners; most of these acquisitions required considerable refitting. Demand for shipping became even more intense as postwar emigration steadily rose, until the United States introduced the 'Quota System', but this did not affect the emigration rate to Canada.

The Cunard Line, which had suffered severely at the hands of the U-boats, ordered three 20,000-tonners; the *Scythia* from Barrow, the *Samaria* from Cammell Laird of Birkenhead, and the *Laconia* from the Tyne. In addition there were three new 14,000-tonners: the *Andania* from Hawthorne Leslie, and the *Antonia* and *Ausonia* from Vickers. They were known as the 'A' liners.

The White Star Line ordered two 16,000-tonners, the *Doric* and *Regina*, from Harland & Wolff of Belfast. The latter, after sailing partly completed as a troopship, was handed over to the Dominion Line and eventually became part of the White Star fleet sailing out of Liverpool mainly to Canada.

The Canadian Pacific Company had acquired the substantial Allen Line fleet during the war, but afterwards most of the Allen vessels were disposed of with the notable exceptions of the *Alsatian*, renamed *Empress of France*, and the *Victorian*, renamed *Marlock*; only the latter ran from Liverpool.

With the restoration of peace the Mersey Docks & Harbour Board was anxious to recommence work at Gladstone without delay. However, the de-commissioning of the great liners had to be accomplished before it could proceed. The Board had to issue a blunt ultimatum to Cunard in February 1921 to remove the *Imperator* from the Dock, as it had decided that it intended to wall-in the entire estate and construct a new lock entrance from the river, with a length of over 1,000 feet to meet the latest shipping requirements. During the period of construction Liverpool was again beset by its old problems of congestion and delay to ships requiring quayside berths.

When completed at a cost of £7.5 million, Gladstone Dock was visited again by King George V and Queen Mary on 19 July 1927. The completed dock proved an enormous asset to the port and its quays were soon occupied by ships of White Star, Canadian Pacific and companies trading to Australasia and the Far East. Canadian Pacific strongly competed with the Cunard and White Star Lines for passengers travelling to Canada. Cunard, which had by 1927 transferred its largest liners to the Southampton service, decided to confine its activities in Liverpool to its traditional berths at Huskisson Dock.

The golden years did not last, as in 1929 came the great Stock Market crash and subsequent economic depression. Shipping was one of the first casualties. Although to some extent the volume of Australian traffic was maintained, Gladstone Dock soon became a haven for laid-up liners owing to the drop in demand for American passages. Very soon both the Cunard and the White Star companies were in serious financial difficulties and, by 1933, they ran alternately each week to share what was left of the Liverpool-New York traffic, with just one ship each to Canada. Only Canadian Pacific seemed able to keep up something comparable to its services of previous years, possibly because this company's financial position was cushioned by large railway and hotel interests in addition to its passenger liners. Some of the laid-up vessels left Gladstone for shipbreakers, sometimes as far away as Japan.

Cunard's prestigious new liner, simply known as No. 534, lay rusting on the stocks at John Brown's shipyard in Glasgow, and Government help was sought to complete it. One of the conditions imposed for such assistance was that the White Star and Cunard Lines should merge to remove wasteful competition, and this was achieved by the passage through Parliament of the North Atlantic Shipping Bill. Unfortunately the majority of the Directors on the Board of the merged company were Cunard men, and the economies that had to be made were usually at White Star's expense. It was not long before the appearance of a White Star liner in Gladstone became rare, and this was particularly so when Cunard White Star took away the motorship *Britannic* to join her newer sister the *Georgic* on the London-Le Havre-Southampton-New York service. Matters at Gladstone Dock improved somewhat, however, when the United States Line commenced a regular transatlantic cargo service using some of the now vacated White Star berths in No 2 Branch.

The enclosing of the graving dock within the extended river wall at Gladstone Dock resulted in a restriction in the turning area needed by vessels requiring to gain entrance from the new 1,050-foot lock from the river, so now only a ship of about 850 feet in length could swing into the graving dock. One of the longest liners to enter Gladstone Graving Dock between the wars was the 722-foot *Mauretania* (II) in 1939. It was hoped that this liner would be sailing regularly from Liverpool to New York, but, after her maiden voyage from the Landing Stage on 17 June, she also joined the service from London, becoming the largest liner to sail up the River Thames and to enter the Surrey Commercial Docks. There was talk of a sister ship, and if the two motorships and the *Mauretania* were brought back to the Mersey, Liverpool might, yet again, have a pre-eminent New York service. Such aspirations were, however, rapidly dispelled by the outbreak of war in 1939.

Right The cessation of hostilities on 11 November 1918 did not lead to the immediate resumption of normal peacetime activities in the port. The Pump Station log (see page 33) shows that the Gladstone Graving Dock was used by a succession of great liners being de-commissioned from wartime employment. December 1918 saw the *Aquitania* in for inspection following her collision with the United States destroyer *Shaw*; at the same time the liner's armaments were removed. It is not known whether her luxurious internal fittings, which had been stored for the duration of the war in the Gladstone's sheds, were replaced at this time or during a later visit.

The Cunard Company decided to convert her to oil fuel, but as the Dock Board did not want to have its main graving dock tied up with a long refit, they exerted considerable influence on Cunard to get the work done elsewhere. Consequently the *Aquitania* went to the Tyne, as seen here, for her major post-war refit.

Below The politicians had promised, as is their wont, that the 1914-18 war was 'the war to end all wars' and that the troops coming home would return to 'a land fit for heroes'. Unfortunately neither promise was kept. Post-war Britain soon found itself enmeshed in economic problems and social unrest. In Liverpool during 1919 there was a police strike and the Government ordered the military to go to the aid of the civil power and ensure the maintenance of law and order. Troops controlled the city centre while a detachment of Royal Marines from the 'R' Class battleship HMS *Revenge*, moored at the Stage, supervised the commercial heart of Liverpool. The local populace do not appear to have been too overawed by the presence of a battleship on their front doorstep.

Above Of the three enormous German liners designed by Albert Ballin, two were at sea when war broke out and the third, the *Bismarck*, was incomplete and all further work had been stopped. The *Imperator* made it back to Germany, while the second ship, *Vaterland*, sought sanctuary and was then interned in New York.

In 1919 the three were confiscated as war reparations. The *Imperator* and the *Vaterland*, which as we have seen had already been seized when the United States entered the war and renamed *Leviathan*, were used by the Americans as troopships. Both made some voyages from Brest, but the Americans required only one so the *Imperator* was laid up in New York and eventually offered to the British Shipping Controller; it was arranged that Cunard would acquire her to replace the sunken *Lusitania*.

The *Imperator* is seen here leaving New York on a misty day *en route* to the Gladstone Dock, which she entered in January 1920 for a quick refit to bring her up to Cunard standards. She made two trips from the Mersey and one from Southampton, but proved to be a very extravagant coal-burner.

Above far right When Cunard decided to keep the *Imperator* in its fleet, she was given a further refit, seen here, in the Gladstone Dock in January 1921. The Dock Board were ready to commence work on the second stage of the Gladstone project and when Cunard announced in February that it was considering extending the refit to include a conversion from coal to oil fuel, the Dock Board decided that it had waited long enough and ordered the *Imperator* out of the graving dock.

Fortunately for Cunard, a notch had been cut in the head of the

Trafalgar Graving Dock at Southampton, so the *Imperator* could just squeeze in. She therefore left Liverpool for the last time and sailed to Southampton, where the refit was completed. The ship was then renamed *Berengaria* and appointed Flagship of the Cunard Fleet. Later in 1921 she was sent up to the Tyne for conversion to oil fuel - the largest liner to berth there.

Although the *Berengaria* was always a difficult ship to man and work, she was selected as the consort to the *Queen Mary* on the transatlantic service until the arrival of the *Queen Elizabeth*. In March 1938 the US Authorities declared her a fire hazard and banned her until she satisfied their safety regulations. Cunard offered her for sale but, not surprisingly, there were no takers. The *Berengaria* then made her second visit to the Tyne where, to ease unemployment in Jarrow, she was partly dismantled; her hull was then scrapped at Inverkeithing.

Right The Aquitania with the Alexandra Towing Company tender alongside is anchored off Woodside waiting her turn to berth at the Landing Stage to enable her passengers to embark; this is evident from the Blue Peter flying from the top of her foremast. She looks in pristine condition after her post-war refit at Swan Hunter's Tyneside yard and at the Gladstone Dock, from which she has just emerged. She was the first merchant ship to be fitted with a Gyro compass after the war. On 17 July 1920 the *Aquitania* left Liverpool on her first refit voyage with all her subsequent sailings being from Southampton. The liner at the Stage is the Dominion Company's *Canada* loading for the St Lawrence. The unusually placid water has enabled the photographer to get a reflection off the Mersey, a rare feat indeed. *C. Heywood*

MARITIME HERITAGE

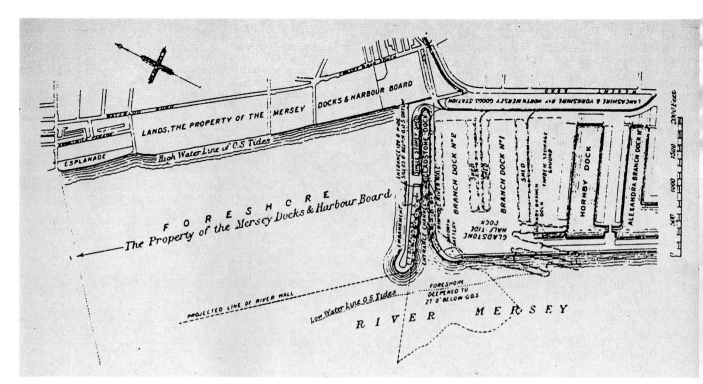

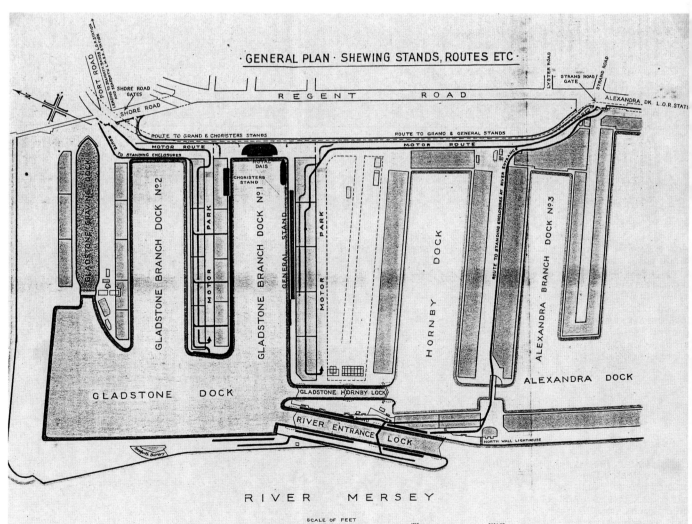

General plan labels: GENERAL PLAN · SHEWING STANDS, ROUTES ETC

Left In February 1921 the Dock Board closed the Gladstone Graving Dock and work resumed to complete the whole estate. With its two deep-water branches and the new river entrance, it was considered to be the largest civil engineering undertaking at the time in the world.

The direct channel to the river had always been considered a temporary arrangement with a short life expectancy, having been designed because of the time limitations before the arrival of the *Aquitania*. The right-angled approach to the Mersey Channel was an unpopular one with mariners, and it was entirely unprotected during stormy conditions, which were usually most prevalent at high water. An oblique approach, facing south, was much pre-ferred, involving a lock system to enable it to be used at all states of the tide.

It came as a considerable shock to Merseyside when it was learned that the graving dock would be included within the boundary of the new estate. This highly imaginative plan of the format that the completed dock was expected to take illustrates the popular impression of those early days. *Mersey Docks & Harbour Board*

Below far left This map, showing how the Gladstone Dock Estate was finally arranged, was produced to guide visitors at the Official Opening in July 1927, and makes an interesting comparison with the previous one. *Mersey Docks & Harbour Board*

PORT OF LIVERPOOL.
PART OF NORTH SYSTEM.

Above The Dock Board took advantage of the post-war opportunity to use aerial photographs in its postcard communications. This one is significant because it shows the Gladstone site under construction in the left foreground, with the lock outline clearly visible. In the background the docks are crammed with ships. The photograph was taken in either late 1921 or early 1922. *C. Heywood*

Right This is the reverse side of the same postcard. The Board must have ordered a large quantity because, as this one proves, they were still being used for official communications as late at July 1928, 12 months after the official opening of the Gladstone Dock. *C. Heywood*

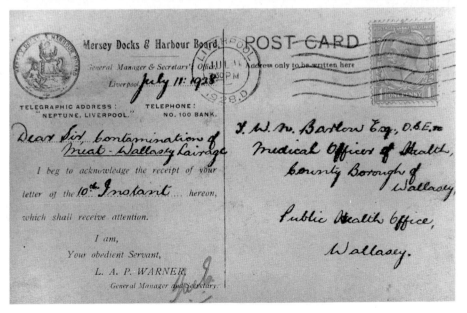

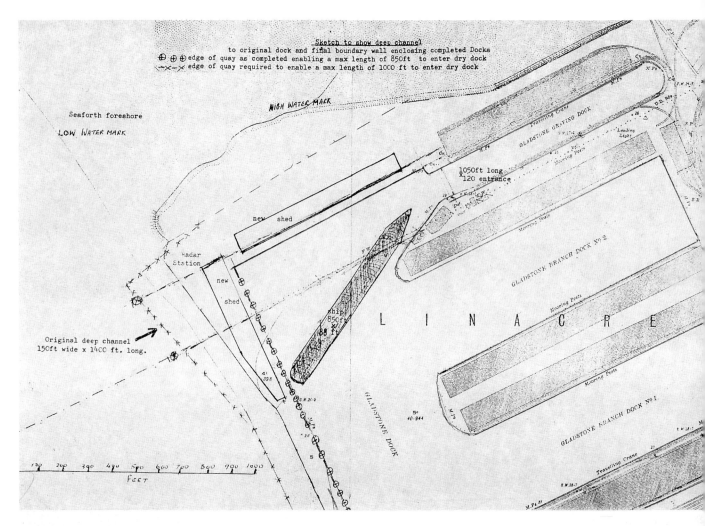

Sketch to show deep channel
to original dock and final boundary wall enclosing completed Docks
⊕ ⊕ ⊕ edge of quay as completed enabling a max length of 850ft to enter dry dock
―×―×― edge of quay required to enable a max length of 1000 ft to enter dry dock

Seaforth foreshore
LOW WATER MARK

HIGH WATER MARK

Radar Station

new shed

new shed

1050ft long
120 entrance

GLADSTONE GRAVING DOCK

Leading Light

Mooring Posts

ship
850ft
× 88 ft

Original deep channel
150ft wide x 1400 ft. long.

GLADSTONE BRANCH DOCK No 2

L I N A C R E

Mooring Posts

GLADSTONE DOCK

GLADSTONE BRANCH DOCK No 1

Travelling Crane

100 200 300 400 500 600 700 800 900 1000
FEET

Above Both the Board and mariners were dissatisfied with the original exposed Entrance Channel making a right-angled connection with the river, and arranged for a 1,070-foot lock facing upstream to take its place. Thus the huge concrete wall on the south side of the channel was partially demolished to form a connection to a wide wall built where the 'dolphins' were sited and to form the base for the Northern transit shed at No 2 Branch. The single original shed was left in situ and sufficient space arranged for a wide roadway with storage space against the wall. Thus it would be possible to walk right round the Graving Dock via the northern and western enclosing walls.

It was, however, generally conceded that there was a blunder over the position of the enclosing wall. This sketch shows that, owing to the close proximity of the wall and the end of No 2 Branch quay, it was now only possible to swing a ship of some 850 feet in length into the 1,000-foot dry dock.

Below By 1922 Gladstone Dock has been closed for completion and the North Docks once again suffered severe congestion. Both ship owners and ship repairers were dismayed when they realised that the graving dock would be out of commission for a considerable time which, of course, brought back all the old pre-war problems of congestion in the North Docks. The loss of revenue to the Dock Board must have been enormous. This view of the Canada and Huskisson estates shows almost all the berths occupied with a most interesting collection of liners. On the west wall at Canada looking from right to left, the first vessel is the Cunarder *Caronia* (the ex-German *Clevelland* and then on charter to White Star as the *Mobile*), and the third is the 12,000-ton *Northland* of the Red Star Line (later to become the *Minnesota* of the United States Atlantic Transport Line). The two-funnelled liner in Canada North is the CPR *Metagama*, with the *Ceramic* in the graving dock. In Huskisson No 3 lies the Dominion liner *Canada*, while in Huskisson No 1 can just be seen the 24,581-ton ex-German *Kaiserin Auguste Victoria* (now named *Express of Scotland*), temporarily on charter to the Cunard Line and about to make a Mediterranean cruise. *C. Heywood*

A PORTION OF THE
MERSEY DOCK ESTATE AT LIVERPOOL

Right The *Doric*, built in 1923 by Harland & Wolff for the White Star's Canadian service, had the distinction of being the only turbine ship the company ever owned. Typical of the immediate post-war design is her cruiser stern, and prominent features are the Topliss davits intended to increase lifeboat accommodation; a legacy of the *Titanic* disaster, they were later removed.

Below right During 1920 Canadian Pacific placed orders for three 16,500-ton liners from the Clyde shipbuilders: the *Montcalm* and *Montclare* from John Brown, and the *Montrose* from Fairfields. To attract more passengers by offering cheaper fares, Canadian Pacific redesignated their accommodation 'Cabin', 'Tourist' and 'Third'. Other companies soon followed suit on their secondary services to New York.

Two of the new 'Monts', as they became popularly known, can be seen here near the Landing Stage, with the *Regina* in the background. Worthy of note is the post-war Canadian Pacific livery that the company adopted in 1920. The *Regina*, which had been ordered by the Dominion Line, was acquired by White Star to run with the *Doric*.

Below Two other fine ships in the Canadian Pacific fleet were the *Melita*, seen here, and the *Minnedosa*. They were partly built on the Clyde, but were then towed to Harland & Wolff's yard at Belfast for completion. They sailed on their maiden voyages to Canada in 1919, but the congestion in Liverpool's docks was so great that they both terminated their voyages at Glasgow after a call at Liverpool Landing Stage.

Above A busy scene at the Landing Stage - the *Baltic* leaves for New York while a Cunard 'A' liner moves to take her place for Canada. Note the White Star tender *Magnetic* in attendance.

Below The sight of two liners loading at the Landing Stage in those busy days was a frequent one. In this view the rear vessel is the Leyland liner *Devonian* (ex-White Star *Cretic*) about to sail for Boston, while ahead of her is Cunard's 20,000-ton *Scythia* sailing between Liverpool and New York. *Liverpool Maritime Museum*

Right The immense scale of the new Gladstone Estate undertaking is readily appreciated in this view of the excavation work in progress. As was the case with the original graving dock, the plans for the second phase were prepared by and the construction work was carried out by the Mersey Docks & Harbour Board's Engineering Department under the direction of the Engineer in Chief, Mr T. M. Newell. Some 12,000,000 tons of clay and sandstone rock had to be excavated during the course of the second phase work, and the walls rose to a height of 63 feet from the dock floor to the quayside. *Mersey Docks & Harbour Board*

Below The completed Gladstone system enclosed a water area of 58¼ acres and had three main quays that provided a total length of over three miles. Minor alterations were also made to the graving dock, which still retained its sliding caisson and powerful pumping station, but the course of the Rimrose Brook had to be altered again, reaching the river more to the south. On the quay three-storey transit sheds were built covering a ground area of 19 acres, with a gross floor area of nearly 60 acres; they had mobile cranes on their flat roofs. These sheds were placed sufficiently well back from the edge of the quays to allow railway tracks to be laid in front of them. Two sets of transit sheds were erected on the central quay, seen here under construction, with a wide roadway between and more railway tracks. The two deep-water loading branches were known as No 1 (South) and No 2 (North). The outer wall also made provision for further handling facilities for ships' cargo, and were known as the West Wall quays, but it was to be some time before further transit sheds were to be built on them. To move cargo the estate was equipped with 49 1½-ton cranes and 17 1-ton cranes supplied by Stothert & Pitt Ltd, Bath, Somerset. *Mersey Docks & Harbour Board*

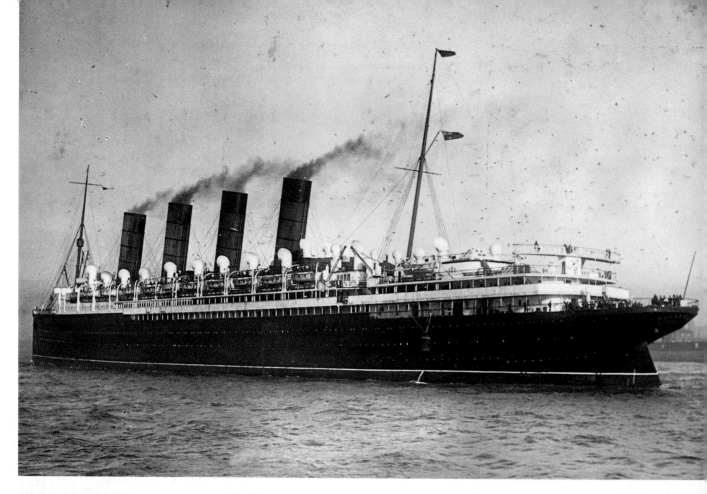

Above On 6 December 1926 the famous *Mauretania* paid her last visit to Liverpool. Unable to arrange accommodation at Southampton for her annual overhaul, she entered Canada Graving Dock once again. At the end of January 1927 she bade farewell to the Mersey and sailed for New York from Southampton at an average speed of 23 knots. Her record voyages at over 25 knots were yet to come.

Below July 1927, and the Gladstone Dock Estate, costing £7,500,000, is finished and, after the Official Opening, ready for business. In the extreme left of the photograph is the distinctive jib of the world's largest floating crane, the 'Mammoth', acquired from the Germans as war reparations.

Also clearly visible is the great lock into the Mersey from the Gladstone Estate, which was one of the largest in the world. It was 1,070 feet long and 130 feet wide, with an interim gate that could be used for smaller vessels. The depth on the sills at normal high water was about 50 feet, at low tide 22 feet, and it was considered that from half tide it could pass the largest ships ever likely to be constructed. Provision for a second entrance alongside it to the north was made but, so far, this has never been constructed. The massive gates, weighing 500 tons each, were moved by hydraulic power and the lock was filled from sluices at various points to prevent surging. No mechanical pumping was deemed necessary.

A further lock was included to connect Gladstone with Hornby and the remainder of the North Docks system, this having dimensions of 645 feet in length and 90 feet in width. *Mersey Docks & Harbour Board*

MARITIME HERITAGE

PROGRAMME.

11-30 a.m.   The Royal train will arrive at the Riverside Station where Their Majesties will be received by:—

The High Sheriff
The Right Hon. The Lord Mayor of Liverpool,
(Lt.-Col. Sir James P. Reynolds, Bart., D.S.O., D.L.)   (Councillor F. C. Bowring).

The Right Hon. The Lady Mayoress, (Mrs. E. W. Hope).
The Earl of Derby, K.G., G.C.V.O., G.C.B., P.C.
The Countess of Derby.

The Right Hon. Sir Archibald T. Salvidge, P.C., K.B.E.
Lt.-General Sir Richard H. K. Butler, K.C.B., K.C.M.G., G.O.C. Western Command.
The Town Clerk of Liverpool, (Mr. Walter Moon).
Commodore Sir Ian Malcolm Bonham-Carter, C.B., C.B.E., Royal Air Force.
The Chief Constable of Liverpool, (Mr. L. D. L. Everett, O.B.E.).
The Chairman of the Mersey Docks and Harbour Board, (Mr. R. D. Holt).
Mrs. Holt.
The General Manager and Secretary of the Board, (Mr. L. A. P. Warner, C.B.E.)

His Majesty will inspect the Guard of Honour furnished by the Royal Naval Volunteer Reserve.

11-35 a.m.   The Lord Mayor and Lady Mayoress, accompanied by Sir Archibald Salvidge and the Town Clerk, will leave for St. George's Hall in order to receive Their Majesties on arrival there.

11-40 a.m.   Their Majesties will leave the Riverside Station for St. George's Hall.

2-20 p.m.   Their Majesties will arrive at No. 7 Bridge, Princes Parade, and will proceed to the Landing Stage where Miss Lois Hurter, Granddaughter of Mr. Thomas Rome, (Chairman of the Board, April 1919-May 1927) will have the honour of presenting a Bouquet to Her Majesty The Queen.

Their Majesties will then embark on the S.S. "Galatea" where they will be received by Mr. Holt, the Chairman of the Mersey Docks and Harbour Board.

2-25 p.m.   The "Galatea" will leave the Landing Stage and proceed down the River to the Gladstone Lock.

The Band of the Training Ship "Indefatigable" will play the National Anthem.

3-5 p.m.   The "Galatea" will enter the Gladstone Lock, breaking the ribbon placed across the entrance.

As the "Galatea" passes through the Lock there will be Community singing of two verses of "Rule Britannia," accompanied by the Band of The Lancashire and National Sea Training Homes.

The "Galatea" will proceed Northward through the Gladstone Dock to enable Their Majesties to see in the distance the Gladstone Graving Dock which they opened in 1913, and will then pass up the Branch Dock, No. 1, to a position at the East end thereof.

Whilst the "Galatea" is passing up the Branch Dock there will be Community singing of Elgar's "Land of Hope and Glory," led by the Choir and accompanied by the Band of the 2nd Battalion, The King's Regiment (Liverpool).

3-20 p.m.   Their Majesties will disembark and the King will inspect the Guard of Honour furnished by the Royal Naval Reserve.

Their Majesties will proceed to the Royal Dais.

As soon as Their Majesties have taken their places on the Royal Dais there will be Community singing of two verses of the National Anthem, led by the Choir and accompanied by the Band of the 2nd Battalion. The King's Regiment (Liverpool).

God Save the King.

God save our gracious King,
Long live our noble King;
God save the King.
Send him victorious,
Happy and glorious,
Long to reign over us,
God save the King.

Thy choicest gifts in store
On him be pleased to pour;
Long may he reign.
May he defend our laws,
And ever give us cause
To sing with heart and voice
God save the King.

Mr. Holt will read an Address to His Majesty from the Mersey Docks and Harbour Board.

His Majesty will read his reply and then declare the Docks open. This will be followed by a fanfare of trumpets.

3-50 p.m.   Their Majesties will leave the Dais to enter their carriage and the first verse of the National Anthem will be sung by all present, led by the Choir and accompanied by the Band of the 2nd Battalion, The King's Regiment (Liverpool).

The Royal Carriage will leave the Dock Estate for Bootle Station by way of the Shore Road Gate.

Above The Gladstone Dock Estate was opened by Their Majesties King George V and Queen Mary on 19 July 1927; this was the programme of events.

Left This time there was no shipping pageant, which had been such a notable feature of the 1913 event, but the Royal Party were once again carried on the *Galatea*. The only ships she sailed past on this occasion were the Ulster ferry *Patriotic* and the White Star liner *Adriatic*. The *Galatea* with the Royal Party aboard is seen here passing the latter outside the Gladstone entrance; it is not recorded how Their Majesties responded to the pall of smoke and soot emanating from the *Adriatic*'s royal salute. The *Galatea*, cheered by thousands of spectators, then steamed through the great lock and broke the ceremonial tape. The Royal Party carried on to No 1 Branch where stands had been erected, and, after the opening ceremony, they motored through the streets of Bootle, packed with cheering spectators, to Oriel Road station to board the Royal Train, which had been brought up from Riverside station. Among the spectators was the author, who as a young boy in the company of his parents dutifully waved his Union Jack as the Royal motor cavalcade passed by.

Above Hard on the stern of the *Galatea* steamed the *Adriatic*, the first liner to enter the new system. She moored in No 2 Branch, which had been given over entirely to ships of the White Star Line. The north side of No 1 Branch became the Canadian Pacific terminal, while the south quay was earmarked for ships of the Blue Funnel Line and those of Geo Thompson & Co sailing to Australia.

Below One of the first ships to use the graving dock was HMS *Rodney*, which came over from Cammell Laird's yard at Birkenhead for hull cleaning before returning there to be commis-

sioned. Together with her sister ship HMS *Nelson*, she had a most unusual and distinctive silhouette, with all nine 16-inch guns mounted forward. Aft of her bridge and funnel she had a very short stern section. The 38,000-ton battleship's design and specifications reflected the restrictions imposed on warship construction by the Washington Treaty following the 1914-18 war; her dimensions were length 710 feet, beam 106 feet, draught 30 feet, with a complement of 1,314. Originally she had been intended to have been a 48,000-ton battleship. She is seen here being manoeuvred out of Cammell Laird's fitting-out basin *en route* to Gladstone Graving Dock.

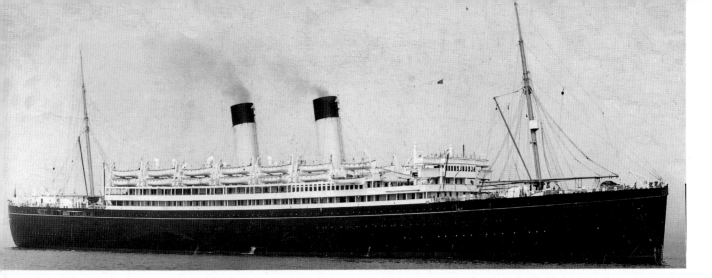

Above On 1 January 1927 the Americans sold the European assets of the International Mercantile Combine. There was, however, in course of construction at Harland & Wolff a liner ordered in 1926 for the White Star Line. She was completed at a strictly limited cost and was even a coal-burner! The 18,724-ton triple-screw *Laurentic* is seen here in the Mersey for her maiden voyage on 11 November 1927. She carried 1,500 passengers: 594 Cabin, 406 Tourist and 500 3rd Class. Since the *Laurentic* had been fitted with telescopic masts in order to pass under the Quebec Bridge she was able to sail to Montreal.

Right In 1928 the Canadian Pacific Company decided to reduce its passenger fleet by disposing of all the tonnage obtained earlier from the merger with the Allen Line and also from the Germans as war reparations. The three 1922 'Monts' were placed on a new Antwerp-Southampton-Canada service while, for Liverpool, four new, almost identical 20,000-ton liners were ordered from the Clyde. They were named after duchesses: the *Duchess of Atholl* (seen here), *Bedford*, *Richmond* and *York*. They were not particularly outstanding vessels and had a reputation for rolling, but, with their efficient turbine propulsion and three-class accommodation, they were well suited to meet the hard times ahead and, having short masts, they could also reach Montreal.

The prospects for Merseyside shipping looked rosy once more now that the regular weekly services to New York and to Canada had established themselves. In addition, Lord Kylsant (Chairman of the Royal Mail Line and also of Harland & Wolff) had managed to buy back the White Star Line from the Americans. As many as four passenger liners left the Gladstone each week to embark passengers at the Landing Stage. Strangely, Cunard did not apply to the Dock Board for space at Gladstone, preferring to continue to use its time-honoured berths at Huskisson.

Right In December 1928 the *Celtic*, whilst returning to Liverpool from New York, hit rocks off Roches Point, Southern Ireland, and became a total loss. To replace her the White Star Company acquired the Royal Mail liner *Ohio* and renamed her *Albertic*. Originally the vessel had been the German liner *Munchen*, but had come into British ownership as a war reparations settlement. The *Albertic* is seen here leaving Gladstone Dock for the Landing Stage to embark passengers for New York. On the left is a CPR 'Mont' waiting at the West Wall for her turn to use the river entrance.

New in 1928, the Canadian Pacific's *Duchess of Bedford* is seen here in No 1 Branch discharging grain into barges by means of a floating elevator.

MARITIME HERITAGE

RMS DEMOSTHENES

Above On the south side of No 1 Branch can be seen the Aberdeen liner *Demosthenes* ready to sail to Australia. This company later amalgamated to form the Aberdeen-White Star Line.

Right Another well-remembered liner that sailed from Liverpool to Australia via the Cape was the 18,495-ton *Ceramic*. She normally berthed in Gladstone No 2 Branch South, and is seen here in the river waiting to enter dock.

Right The Gladstone River Entrance at high water with a White Star Liner *en route* to the Landing Stage for passengers.

LIVERPOOL AND THE MERSEY

Above The connecting lock from Gladstone into Hornby provided a very useful access to the river for traffic from Hornby, Alexandra, and Brocklebank Docks. Here a Clan Line liner, *Clan MacTaggart*, is seen passing through the connecting lock *en route* to the company's berth at Alexandra Dock.

Below Another company that welcomed the new connection was the Furness-Withy Line. Their 6,800-ton vessels, the *Newfoundland* (seen here) and *Nova Scotia*, were delivered in 1925 and 1926 respectively. They had accommodation for only 185 passengers and, to avoid delay, seldom used the Landing Stage. Hitherto to reach the company's berth at Hornby they would have used the Sandon river entrance, but now the new Hornby Passage offered a more direct and easier alternative route to and from the River Mersey.

MARITIME HERITAGE

In 1927 the White Star Line was purchased from the Americans by Lord Kylsant's Royal Mail Group, which was in financial difficulties due to competition from foreign interests, especially on the South American services. It was hoped that the White Star assets would greatly assist Royal Mail to become more viable. Lord Kylsant was also the Chairman of Harland & Wolff, the Belfast shipbuilders, who had a valuable franchise with the German firm of Burmeister & Wain. This firm specialised in the manufacture of diesel engines for large ships.

Following the merger two liners were transferred from the Royal Mail Line to the White Star; one was the *Ohio*, renamed *Albertic* and seen here (*above*) in White Star colours. As previously stated this was the former German *Munchen* of 19,000 tons, which had replaced the stricken *Celtic* on the Liverpool-New York service.

The other was the *Orca*, renamed *Calgaric* in the White Star fleet. In 1918 this ship had been partially completed for wartime trooping but was subsequently sent back to Harland & Wolff for 'rebuilding' as a passenger liner. She made one voyage from Liverpool in 1929, afterwards transferring to the London-Canada service. She returned to the Mersey in the early 1930s for cheap cruises, and is seen in the second picture berthing at the Landing Stage in 1929.

Above In direct competition with the CPR and Cunard Line's services to Canada, White Star decided to increase its Quebec sailings. The 1909 *Megantic* was transferred from chartered trooping and placed on the Le Havre-Southampton-Canada run, offering Cabin Class accommodation. Early in 1930 she was back in Liverpool and is seen here discharging grain in Gladstone Dock. Both White Star and CPR ships brought back large cargoes of Canadian grain for Merseyside mills. *Mersey Docks & Harbour Board*

Below The Liverpool Overhead Railway line passed within a stone's throw of the Gladstone's quayside sheds, yet the dockers and ships' crews had to use either Seaforth Sands or Alexandra Dock stations to get to and from work. The trek on a rainy windswept day must have tested to the limit the colourful vocabulary of the trudgers.

It was therefore a matter of considerable relief when the Overhead Railway opened a new station at the Gladstone Dock on 16 June 1930. The LOR appreciated the passenger demand for this station because it had the distinction of being the only station on the line provided with two overbridges. The proximity of the dock sheds is quite evident. *Liverpool Overhead Railway*

Above Unfortunately, soon after the Gladstone Dock was opened again the Great Depression began in 1929. Lord Kylsant had by now amassed an enormous shipping 'empire', of which the largest units were Royal Mail and Pacific Steam Navigation. When he bought back White Star from American interests in 1927, he received great public acclaim in Britain. Regrettably he used the White Star asset to prop up his ailing Royal Mail Line and the fall-off in passengers to the United States had its effect. No 2 Branch became a laying-up berth for White Star liners surplus to requirements. However, Kylsant was a great optimist and was of the opinion that the slump would not last and ordered a new ship for White Star in 1930. She was a motorship of 26,943 tons and her new method of propulsion proved to be extremely economical, making her a great favourite with Liverpool people. The new *Britannic* is seen here in No 2 Branch, but ahead of her lies the sad sight of two White Star liners laid up, doing nothing.

Below This 1931 view from the Overhead Railway shows Gladstone Dock No 2 Branch on the left, presenting a dismal scene of the deepening Depression with several White Star liners idle with covers over their funnels.

Despite the slump Canadian Pacific went ahead with its new *Empress of Britain*, seen on the right, which arrived in the graving dock for hull painting after completing her trials. She had been built by John Brown on Clydebank and was of massive proportions - 42,350 tons and capable of carrying 1,182 passengers in three classes.

Shortly afterwards the new liner left for Southampton in order to prepare for her maiden voyage. On the trip down to Southampton she carried a party of invited guests - it is said that there never was a more opulent and lavish positioning voyage. She commenced an express mail service to Quebec on 27 May 1931.
Mersey Docks & Harbour Board

Further endorsing Lord Kylsant's optimism, another new motorship came out of Harland & Wolff's yard in 1932 - the 27,759-ton *Georgic*. She is seen here, when new, docking in Gladstone No 2 Branch. Her public rooms were later thrown open to public viewing and people marvelled at the 'ultra-modern' decor. Unfortunately there proved to be insufficient passenger trade to justify sailing two new motorships from Liverpool, and after her maiden voyage on 26 June 1932 the *Georgic* was transferred to Southampton.

A dock is not the most likely venue for a high society ball, but Gladstone Dock achieved that distinction on Wednesday 19 October 1932. Tickets for the British Legion's 'Derby House' Ball were not cheap, for at that time 25 shillings represented a significant amount of money, for example it was the weekly wage of an unskilled worker. One wonders what were the comments and observations of the Gladstone Dock gateman on 25 bob a week as the local notaries, socialites and celebrities went past him on their way to the *Georgic*. C. Heywood

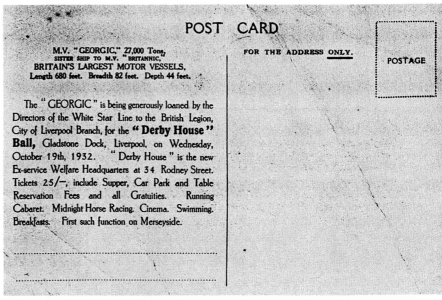

Another view of the *Georgic* in Gladstone No 2 Branch. In the background can be seen the quarterdeck of HMS *Royal Oak* which at the time was on a visit to Liverpool and open to the public.

In the mid-1930s, when the Depression was at its worst, even the usually prosperous Canadian Pacific was unable to find full employment for its 'Duchess' fleet. Here, in Gladstone No 1 branch, we see three of them idle during the winter when the St Lawrence river was frozen.

The Great Shipping Slump lasted until the later 1930s and many lines operating to both North and South America, Australia and the Near East went out of business and their liner fleets were sold. Liverpool was particularly hard hit when Cunard and White Star shared the weekly sailing to New York - few Americans had enough money now to make regular crossings to Europe. The *Britannic, Scythia, Adriatic* and *Samaria* were operating the Boston and New York service. and only the *Laurentic* and *Antonia* were running to Montreal. Canadian Pacific seemed more able to weather the storm with their railway and hotel activities, but even they had to lay up some 'Duchesses' during the winter season.

In 1931 the Kylsant empire crashed, and he was prosecuted for issuing false statements to ward off the creditors. The White Star Line was placed in receivership.

In 1934 Parliament passed the North Atlantic Shipping Bill. This would enable subsidy to be given to Cunard to complete a liner presently on the stocks in John Brown's Clydebank yard. This was 'No 534', destined to become the prestigious *Queen Mary*. However, as a condition of the Government's financial assistance the legislation required Cunard and White Star to merge and thus cut down wasteful competition. As has already been mentioned, because the new Cunard-White Star Board had a preponderance of Cunard Directors, not surprisingly it was the White Star ships that were the ones to be disposed of as soon as possible. An exception was to be made for the two recently constructed motorships.

It was cruising that ultimately came to the rescue of the ship-owners, and the Mersey soon became a much brighter scene with liners, decorated by bunting, waiting in the river for their turn at the Landing Stage to embark holidaymakers on cruises to the Atlantic Isles, the Mediterranean, the West Indies and Norway, some for as little as £1 per day! Two new visitors, resplendent in white-painted hulls, arrived from a prolonged lay-up. These were the Lamport & Holt ships the *Voltaire* and *Vandyck*. Other visitors were the White Star's *Calgaric* and *Adriatic*, the Cunard liners *Lancastria* and *Carinthia* and one of the Canadian Pacific 'Monts'. With the regular New York and Canada sailings it was again possible to see as many as six large liners in the Mersey on a busy weekend.

The *Voltaire* (seen here) and *Vandyck* were 13,200-ton liners assigned to the Lamport & Holt 'V' fleet running between New York and South America. When the *Vestris* foundered on 12 November 1928 the service collapsed and the *Voltaire* and *Vandyck* were laid up. However, the emergence of a cruise trade brought them out to be refitted and painted white for cheap cruising out of Liverpool and they became very popular vessels. Both were subsequently lost in the war; the *Voltaire* was sunk by a German surface raider and the *Vandyck* by a U-boat.

Normally based at Gladstone Dock, the *Vandyck* is seen preparing to enter the river for another 'Holiday in the Sun' - even the tugs are bedecked in festive apparel. One of the more hazardous occupations in the docks was the manning of the 'gig' boats, two of which are clearly visible. Their purpose was to collect and pass over the tow ropes to the tugs, and the mooring lines to the dockers, when vessels were manoeuvring in the docks.

The *Vandyck*, after being repainted as a cruise liner, is approaching the Landing Stage to embark passengers anxious to take advantage of the cheap cruises on offer. In the background is a homeward-bound liner coming up-river.

MARITIME HERITAGE

Above The 16,250-ton *Lancastria* was originally intended to be the *Tyrhenia* for the Anchor Line and became an odd unit in the Cunard fleet. After renaming she was converted to a 'Cabin' Class ship and was, at first, painted white for cruising. She remained cruising until 'called up' for Government service, then made several voyages trooping. On 17 June 1940 she was bombed and sunk off St Nazaire, an event that ranks as Britain's worst maritime disaster as some 3,000 troops and civilians perished.

Below A considerable sum was spent on making the *Adriatic* a more attractive cruise ship for the 1933 season. However, because she was still a coal-burner, it is doubtful whether she turned out to be a paying proposition. She is seen here laid up at the end of the 1933 season, in the almost deserted No 2 Branch. At this time the White Star Line had taken over the whole of No 2 Branch, while the CPR used No 1 Branch North. Alfred Holt's Blue Funnel liners used No 1 Branch East when inward-bound.

One of Liverpool's best-known liners was Cunard's *Scythia*, which had been built at Vickers, Barrow, in 1920; she is seen here in the river. The Cunarders still left on the Liverpool-America service were the *Laconia*, *Scythia* and *Samaria*, with the only remaining 'A' liner, *Antonia*, sailing to Canada. Besides the regular Cunard sailings, other transatlantic departures could be seen on Fridays: one of the 'Duchess' liners to Canada, and the *Laurentic*, the only White Star liner still regularly used on the transatlantic service. On Saturdays there was still the traditional mail departure to New York by one of the Cunarders or by the new *Britannic*. The Donaldson Atlantic Company's 13,500-ton ships *Athenia* and *Letitia* picked up their passengers every other Saturday by tender off New Brighton.

The two remaining White Star liners, *Doric*, built in 1925, and *Laurentic*, built in 1927, were familiar sights on the Mersey. The *Laurentic* is seen here being manoeuvred out of the Gladstone lock by the White Star tender *Magnetic*. Both liners subsequently had chequered careers. In September 1935 the *Doric* was in collision with the French liner *Formigny* off Cape Finisterre, and was then scrapped at Newport, Monmouthshire, at the end of the year.

In August 1935 the *Laurentic* collided with the *Napier Star* and managed to limp back to the Gladstone where she was repaired then laid up in the Bidston Dock at Birkenhead. On the outbreak of the Second World War in 1939 she was commandeered by the Government for trooping, then after the Dunkirk evacuation she was converted into an Armed Merchant Cruiser. On 3 November 1940 she was sunk by *U-99* 40 miles to the west of Bloody Foreland, in the northwest corner of Ireland.

Another liner is leaving Liverpool for the last time. After only one season cruising the *Adriatic* was sold to the Japanese for scrap. She is seen here leaving Gladstone Dock on 19 December 1934 sailing to the Far East under her own steam - still burning coal.

MARITIME HERITAGE

Above The decision to reduce the former White Star fleet meant that by 1935 only the *Britannic* and the *Georgic* were still sailing in White Star colours. Throughout the lives of these two liners their crews displayed loyalty to their old company by ensuring that the White Star pennant always flew above that of Cunard, irrespective of the balance of power on the Board of Directors.

In April 1935 the Cunard-White Star Board decided to take the *Britannic* from the Mersey to join her sister ship, the *Georgic*, on the London-Le Havre-Southampton-New York service. The *Britannic* is seen here at the Stage prior to her transfer to Southampton. Following in the wake of the original transfer of the *Georgic*, this was a serious setback for Liverpool.

Right A typical mid-week scene on the Mersey in the summer of 1935. The new Isle of Man steamer *Mona's Queen* is about to sail for Douglas while a CPR 'Mont', possibly deputising for a 'Duchess' on the weekly Canadian service, is on her way from the Gladstone to embark her passengers at the Stage.

In November 1938 Britain's first purpose-built aircraft carrier, HMS *Ark Royal*, was completed by Cammell Laird and was then brought across the Mersey to the Gladstone Graving Dock for hull painting. She caused enormous interest on Merseyside. With a displacement of 27,000 tons when fully loaded and a complement of 1,575 men and 60 operational aircraft, she was impressive by any standards. *Ark Royal*'s dimensions were 800 feet long, 95 feet in the beam and 22 feet draught, so it was quite a spectacular occasion when she was put into the graving dock; here she is seen passing through the great lock at high tide. In the first two years of the Second World War German propagandists claimed to have sunk the *Ark Royal* more times than any other British warship, such was her fame. However, one such claim proved to be true when, in November 1941 while in the Mediterranean under tow to Gibraltar, the *Ark Royal* came under U-boat attack and subsequently sank. Her loss saddened many hearts on Merseyside. *S. Bale*

MARITIME HERITAGE

A new Cunard liner, the 35,655-ton *Mauretania* (II), was launched at Cammell Laird's shipyard on 28 July 1938. In May 1939 she was moved to the Gladstone Graving Dock for a final coat of paint. Many Merseysiders had great hopes that the new liner would do much to boost the port's reputation as a passenger terminal. If the *Britannic* and *Georgic* came back to join the new *Mauretania* in a three-ship service to New York, then Liverpool would, once again, be able to boast of having a first-class transatlantic service. Those aspirations were, however, short-lived. On 17 June 1939 the *Mauretania* left the Stage on her maiden voyage to New York, and she was then transferred to London to join the motor ships on the Le Havre-Southampton-New York service, becoming the largest passenger liner ever to use the Surrey Commercial Docks at London. *S. Bale*

Manoeuvring the _Mauretania_ around the knuckle in order to enter the Gladstone Graving Dock required expertise of the highest order. An appreciative audience has gathered to watch the proceedings. _S. Bale_

Above There had been plans for the giant *Empress of Britain* to have a sister ship for a new super service between Southampton and Quebec. However, the economic depression made this impossible so the *Empress of Australia* was refitted instead and painted white. The service continued successfully for six years and, during the winter when the St Lawrence was frozen over, the ships went on world cruises.

In 1939 it was decided to use the ships for a State Visit by Their Majesties King George VI and Queen Elizabeth to Canada and the USA. On 6 May the *Empress of Australia* would take them from Portsmouth to Canada, and on 17 June the *Empress of Britain* would bring them back to Southampton from America.

The *Empress of Australia*'s bow section is seen here early in 1939 at Gladstone's West Wall awaiting attention prior to the outward voyage. The Vulcan Foundry-built railway locomotive is awaiting export, appropriately to Australia, and stands on one of the multi-tracks at Gladstone.

Right On Saturday 2 September 1939 war was once again imminent and barrage balloons hung grotesquely over the port just in case German bombers made a surprise attack. All shipping was at a standstill except for one vessel, the Donaldson Atlantic Company's liner *Athenia*. Because the Landing Stage was normally occupied by a succession of transatlantic and cruise liners on a summer Saturday, it was customary for the Donaldson ships to pick up their passengers by tender in the river between Gladstone and New Brighton. But on that Saturday, the day before war broke out, the *Athenia* had no difficulty in finding room at the Stage, as this photograph shows. Among her passengers were a number of Americans anxious to get home while sailing tickets were still available.

The River Mersey was unnervingly quiet as the *Athenia* left Liverpool on that fateful Saturday and proceeded to Belfast. After that call, and with a record number of passengers on board, she faced the broad Atlantic *en route* to the St Lawrence. During the night she was fully blacked out, but early on Monday 4 September when about 250 miles to the north-west of Rathin Island, she was observed by the captain of the *U-30*. He claimed later that he thought she was a warship and, consequently, sank her with two torpedoes; 112 passengers and crewmen of the *Athenia* were lost. There was to be no 'phoney war' at sea; the people of Liverpool realised that the war at sea commenced the weekend war broke out.

4. THE SECOND WORLD WAR 1939-45

When the *Athenia* sailed from Liverpool on 2 September 1939 the Mersey seemed strangely deserted for a Saturday, but when the Second World War got into its stride things became vastly different. At sea there was no 'phoney war' period, and convoys began almost immediately with the Mersey estuary becoming one of the great assembly and arrival points for the ships. Ferryboat passengers were presented with a never-ending panorama of ships of all types and sizes at anchor awaiting their sailing orders, and hardly a day went by when a liner could not be seen embarking troops at the Landing Stage. After the fall of France in 1940, when both London and Southampton were deemed too dangerous for large ships, many strangers arrived in the Mersey, ships that would never have come to Liverpool in normal times.

With the exception of the two 'Queens', almost every large liner serving the Allied cause - American, Dutch and French - arrived, while the catalogue of naval vessels read like *Jane's Fighting Ships*, the larger ones usually entering Gladstone Dock.

Victory at sea was crucial, not only to the overall war effort, but for Britain's very survival. It has been asserted by military experts that the Clyde and the Mersey, and in particular the Gladstone Dock, did more to bring us victory than any other facilities used during the war. Liverpool's naval base on the West Wall at Gladstone supplied most of the convoy escorts in the form of destroyers, sloops and corvettes, and the exploits of the famous 'hunter-killer' flotilla under the command of Captain Walker will never be forgotten.

The *Monarch of Bermuda*, 22,420 tons, was built in 1931 by Vickers on the Tyne for Furness Withy's 'millionaire's run' between New York and Bermuda.

In November 1939 she came to Cammell Laird's shipyard in Birkenhead for conversion into a troop transport. The prominent ventilators were fitted by Laird's to improve the air supply to the troop decks.

Until mid-1942 the *Monarch of Bermuda* was also equipped as an Armed Merchant Cruiser and she is seen here flying the white ensign with her aft armament clearly visible. The location of this photograph is not certain, but the presence of an anti-torpedo boom would suggest either Scapa or the estuary of the Clyde. During the war the *Monarch of Bermuda* was a regular visitor to the Mersey as a troop transport. Throughout her war service she retained three funnels, unlike her sister ship the *Queen of Bermuda*, whose funnels were reduced to two.

Above As long ago as 1936 the Port Emergency Committee had been formed in case there was another world conflict, and Liverpool's strategic position made it an obvious choice for both the assembly and reception of convoys. Merseyside's great asset was the Gladstone Dock with its deep-water quays and fine river entrance. With the outbreak of war the dockland scene changed overnight. Quays had to be kept clear and the docks became a forbidden area to all except those who were given official permission to be there.

Initially, there were two main concerns: maintaining the 'blackout' and arranging for all seagoing vessels to be painted overall in grey in order to conceal their identity and to obscure their presence when at sea. The Mersey soon began to take on a warlike appearance. Ships of the Royal Navy, normally a rare sight in Liverpool, arrived as escorts for the convoys. For this purpose mainly destroyers and sloops were employed. At first they were based in Birkenhead Docks, but then a naval base was established on the West Wall of Gladstone Dock and soon acquired the nickname 'The Flotilla Club'.

At the commencement of hostilities all voyages by deep-sea ships were cancelled and the movement of vessels came under the control of the Ministry of Shipping after the sinking of the *Athenia*. Incoming ships did not sail again until convoys for them had been arranged, and the convoys assembled in the river, as this scene shows. *Imperial War Museum*

Below The *Mauretania*, after being held for a time in New York, was now back in the Gladstone for conversion to war duties. Opposite her and already repainted in wartime grey is the *Empress of Japan*, flagship of the CPR fleet.

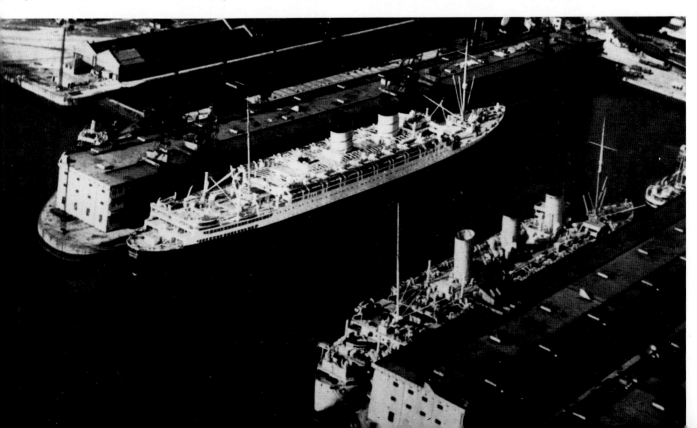

Another early wartime arrival in the Gladstone Graving Dock was the *Empress of Britain*. At that time powerful searchlights on the Perch Rock New Brighton Battery panned around the estuary of the Mersey whenever enemy aircraft approached to check that no mines had been dropped. This produced considerable apprehension among the residents of Bootle, because the great bulk of the *Empress of Britain* was brought into stark relief in the sweep of the powerful searchlights, presenting an inviting target for German bomb-aimers. If the bombs missed, their homes would 'cop it'.

Above Once again, as in 1914, the Mersey became a very busy river indeed. Most of the naval activity was to be found at Gladstone Dock, but many passenger liners were requisitioned as transports to carry forces overseas. The convoy system had been introduced at the beginning of the conflict and liners, fully loaded, were frequently to be seen at anchor in the Mersey awaiting their sailing orders. There were many strangers - ships that in normal times would never have sailed from Liverpool - and typical examples were Furness Withy's two super luxury ships from the New York-Bermuda service, the *Monarch of Bermuda* and *Queen of Bermuda*. In this view, taken from an aircraft of Coastal Command, the former, doing service as a troopship, is in company with the *Empress of Australia* as part of a fast convoy leaving the Mersey estuary.

Below HMS *Barham* was the first large naval unit to arrive at Liverpool. Between the wars the 'Super Dreadnought' had been redesigned and now had one funnel only. She had suffered an underwater explosion in 1940 and was brought for repairs to Gladstone Dock, where she remained for a considerable period. The end of the *Barham* is often seen in television war documentaries. A cine-photographer happened to be filming as the battleship, while under way in the Mediterranean, was torpedoed, slowly began to heel over and, when almost horizontal, blew up in a tremendous explosion.

Left In 1940 there was a Government-sponsored scheme for the evacuation of children to the colonies, provided that their parents could afford the passage. Both the Dutch liner *Volendam* and Ellerman's two-funnelled *City of Benares* seen here, sailed from Liverpool *en route* for Canada. The *Volendam* was torpedoed, but managed to put back to the Clyde; however, the *City of Benares* sank with heavy casualties. After this the scheme was abandoned.

Below left In May 1940 HMS *Hood* was escorted from Devonport to Gladstone Dock to complete her refit. At 860 feet she was the longest ship to enter the graving dock. It must have given the Dockmaster some anxious moments as her starboard side cleared by inches the knuckle at the west end of No 2 Branch.

The *Hood* was the pride of the Royal Navy and was often referred to as 'The Mighty Hood'. The 46,300-ton battleship mounted eight 15-inch and 12 5.5-inch guns, and could exceed 32 knots. She was 105 feet in the beam and had a draught 31 feet. During the engagement with the *Bismarck* the *Hood*'s magazine was hit and only three out of the ship's complement of 1,341 survived the explosion.

Below On 12 June 1940 the *Hood* put to sea to meet one of the greatest convoys of the war; it included the *Queen Mary*, *Aquitania*, *Empress of Britain*, *Mauretania*, *Andes* and *Empress of Canada*. The *Queen Mary* went to the Clyde, and the Mersey received the rest; for the first time in 20 years a four-stacker was back in the river. Space was at a premium and the Gladstone could only accommodate the *Aquitania*; the escort flotillas had to find berths in Hornby and Alexandra Docks, while the great liner took over the West Wall where she lay in the mist like a grey ghost from the past. In February 1941 the *Aquitania* sailed from Liverpool in an Express Convoy bound for Australia, seen here overwatched by the crew of a Coastal Command aircraft.

Some idea of the massive congestion in the Docks on both sides of the Mersey can be grasped from this well-known photograph. Pictures of shipping in dock during wartime are rare for security reasons, and this view brings out the difficulty of identifying vessels when their names have been removed and they are all painted in one shade of grey. It is of interest to note that each of the merchant ships is defensively armed usually with a bow gun emplacement, which would be manned by army gunners. This view was taken from Huskisson No 3 Branch looking across towards the river wall at Canada Dock. *Mersey Docks & Harbour Board*

The fall of France made both the Thames and the Solent too dangerous for large ships; consequently almost the entire burden of the war at sea fell on the Clyde and the Mersey. Liverpool had by far the better dock system, as Glasgow's was situated on the upper Clyde beyond the narrows, making it necessary to load and unload troopships by tenders from either Gourock or Greenock.

When the French capitulated, the *Ile de France* managed to escape capture and joined the Allied cause. So the Mersey saw the arrival of yet another stranger. She was the second longest ship, at 764 feet, to enter the Gladstone Graving Dock and must have given the Dockmaster nearly as many problems as the *Hood*.

Another French escapee was the 28,000-ton liner *Pasteur*, built in 1938 for the South American service. During the war she was managed by Cunard, but afterwards she was handed back to the French and in 1957 was purchased by the Germans. The liner was sold to the Saudis in 1977 for use as a floating hotel at Jedda. Finally, in 1980, she sank while under tow on the way to Taiwan for scrapping.

Left One serious casualty of the German bombardment was the new HMS *Prince of Wales*. During an air raid in 1940, while in the fitting-out basin in Cammell Laird's shipyard in Birkenhead, a bomb dropped between the quayside and the stern section of the battleship, damaging one of her turrets and delaying completion.

The 35,000-ton *Prince of Wales* was one of the 'King George V' class of battleships, and had a complement of 1,500. Her dimensions were a length of 740 feet, beam 103 feet and draught 27 feet. Her armaments included ten 14-inch and 16 5.25-inch guns. This rare view shows her on trials during 1940 in the Irish Sea in weather not untypical for this part of the world. To repair the bomb damage her aft crane has been temporarily removed, as have the gun barrels of her rear main armament.

When the *Prince of Wales* joined in the pursuit of the *Bismarck*, Cammell Laird workmen were still on board. Not surprisingly they demanded danger money on completion of their adventurous voyage, but it is not known whether they actually received any. She had to disengage because of problems with her main armament.

On 8 December 1941 HMS *Prince of Wales* and the battle cruiser HMS *Repulse* were sunk by a Japanese aircraft in the South China Sea off the Malayan Peninsula. This demonstrated that the era of the battleship as lord of the seas was over. From then on capital ships, to operate effectively and safely, needed air cover to protect them from their vulnerability to air attack.

Middle left In the cellar of Derby House was established the top secret Headquarters of Western Approaches Command, the best-known Commander of which was the charismatic Admiral, Sir Max Horton. The 'Battle of the Atlantic' was directed from here for nearly five years - on large wall-maps were plotted the position of all inward- and outward-bound convoys together with the known or suspected disposition of enemy forces. The struggle was titanic, remorseless and unrelenting from the very first to the very last day of the war. *Imperial War Museum*

Left Naval attacks against U-boats were usually conducted at a distance - by depth-charging and occasionally by gunfire. Encounters of a closer kind always caught the imagination of the public. The ramming of a U-boat required outstanding qualities of daring leadership and skilful seamanship, and the return of an escort vessel with that unmistakeable dent in her bow demonstrated an incontrovertible 'kill'. Such achievements were accorded special recognition and appreciation, as seen here.

Above The arrival of the small 'Flower' Class corvettes did much to ease the burden of the escorts. They could be built quickly and were provided with a single 6-inch gun, depth-charges and asdic. They were soon equipped with the new 271 type 10 cm radar scanners, which proved to be one of the main factors that won the Battle of the Atlantic. It was also placed on the bridge of many liners and can be identified by the 'lighthouse'-type structure ahead of the funnels.

Below The exploits of the Liverpool Escort Group will always be associated with the name of Captain Johnny Walker, who was given a flotilla of sloops working as a freelance 'hunter-killer' unit acting on direct orders from Derby House. On one sortie Walker's flotilla sank six U-boats and, on his return, the entire workforce at Gladstone Dock stopped work and went to the Great Lock to cheer him in.

MARITIME HERITAC

Right The occupation of Northern France and of the Low Countries brought the North West of England within the range of German bombers, so air raids became a regular feature of wartime existence. In May 1941 the Germans launched a series of concentrated air attacks on Liverpool, the purpose of which was to destroy the docks, render the port useless, and to break the morale of the people. The May 'Blitz' lasted for over a week. The city centre was largely destroyed and, although a number of ships were sunk in the river and in the docks, including two in the Gladstone, none of the German objectives was achieved. Efforts were made to close Gladstone Dock by hitting the river entrance and immobilising the Great Lock, but only the west end of No 1 South transit shed was damaged, seen here, and the Dock continued to function. *Mersey Docks & Harbour Board*

Below The large liners continued to arrive bringing troops from Australia, New Zealand, Canada and America. Here at the Stage can be seen the *Empress of Australia* and *Empress of Scotland*. The latter had been the *Empress of Japan*, but after the surprise attack on Pearl Harbor, her name was hastily changed. When they were ready for the next voyage, the liners loaded at the Landing Stage, often with RAF personnel from the depots at West Kirby, Blackpool and Cosford, and they would then have to wait, sometimes for days, in the River Mersey waiting to join a convoy, with the troops having little to do except admire the girls on the passing ferries. Noteworthy is the bomb-damaged roof of the Riverside station; a troop train can be seen in the platform.

One ship that sailed regularly from Gladstone via the Cape to Australia with both passengers and troops was the ex-White Star *Ceramic*, by then part of the Shaw Savill Fleet. Once clear of home waters she sailed unescorted, but at the end of 1942 failed to reach her destination. Her fate was unknown until the war was over and a prisoner-of-war revealed what had happened. On 6 December 1942 the *Ceramic* was sunk by *U-515*. The prisoner proved to be the sole survivor from 656 people on board, having been clutched from the sea and taken to Germany as evidence of yet another sinking.

The *Queen of Bermuda* is seen at anchor in the River Mersey in her wartime livery. Her aft funnel was removed by Harland & Wolff at Belfast to make way for the installation of a battery of anti-aircraft guns, and the radar 'lighthouse' in front of her mast is clearly visible.

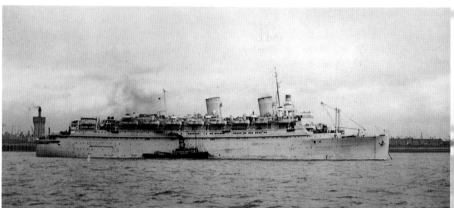

In the build-up to the D-day landings reinforcements poured across the Atlantic. Another troopship that made several voyages to Liverpool was the *Dominion Monarch*, seen here approaching the Stage.

MARITIME HERITAGE

Above Early in 1943 a very woe-begone-looking liner arrived in Liverpool. She was the *Georgic*, which had been set on fire and sunk during an air raid on Port Tewfik, Suez, on 14 July 1941. She was refloated and, in the following December, was towed by the *Clan Campbell* and *City of Sydney* to Port Sudan. A further tow by the *Haresfield* and *Recorder* took her to Karachi where her engines were reconditioned. She then returned to Liverpool under her own power. When she was examined in the Gladstone Graving Dock, the Admiralty decided that their need to have the dock readily available was a greater priority, so the vessel was sent to Belfast for a protracted major refit. Here the *Georgic* is seen after re-entering service as a troopship in 1944.

Right When the *Aquitania* left, the Escort Groups returned to Gladstone's West Wall. HMS *Starling*, on the left, and HMS *Wildgoose* are in the Great Lock outward-bound on yet another sortie.

Below right The invasion of Russia in June 1941 meant that much of the Luftwaffe's air power was diverted to the Eastern Front. Consequently the intense and sustained bombing of British cities ceased, so Liverpool did not experience a repetition of the May 'Blitz'. Air raids continued to occur periodically, but as Allied air power increased and air defences improved, the Germans resorted to making surprise raids by single aircraft on particular targets. Ports were especially susceptible to surprise low-level air attacks coming in over the sea, so Sea Forts were erected in the sea approaches and river estuaries of Britain's major ports. The forts were equipped with the latest radar equipment and bristled with anti-aircraft guns. Because Merseyside and, in particular on account of its location, Gladstone Dock were vulnerable to this type of attack, a cluster of Sea Forts was erected off the Formby Channel, the main sea approach to Liverpool.

Above Liners, both British and foreign, were used by the Allies as hospital ships. The 24,370-ton *Oranje* escaped from Holland and served with the Royal Australian Navy as a hospital ship. She is seen here on one of her visits to the Mersey, with the *Mauretania* at the Landing Stage. After the war she became the cruise ship *Angelina Lauro*; she was gutted by fire at St Thomas in 1979 and sank while under tow in the Pacific.

Below Huge quantities of equipment passed through the port in the preparations for the invasion of Europe. Cargo space was filled by every conceivable type of equipment from aircraft in crates and complete railway engines to Landing Craft, as seen here. Much use was made of the Dock Board's floating crane, 'Mammoth', here at work in Gladstone Dock. *Mersey Docks & Harbour Board*

Later the Americans were back, and the transport ship *Wakefield* is seen in the river. She was originally the United States Line's *Manhattan* (24,218 tons) and, when America entered the war, was refitted for trooping. On 3 September 1942 a disastrous fire broke out and the blazing ship was towed to Halifax where it was extinguished. She was then towed to Boston and it was 4 April 1944 before she was able to sail again. The *Wakefield*, her profile now greatly altered, made 23 Atlantic round trips between Liverpool and Boston. After war service she was laid up in the Hudson until scrapped in 1964.

With the exception of the two giant 'Queens', there cannot have been many liners sailing for the Allies that did not come to the Mersey at some time during the war.

Had it not been for the war, the *Stirling Castle* would not normally have come into Liverpool. She is seen here in wartime grey approaching the Landing Stage in order to disembark more troops.

'You'll get no promotion this side of the ocean, so cheer up my lads, bless them all' was a refrain familiar to many forces personnel in the Second World War. These American troops disembarking from the *Stirling Castle* at the Stage had their own version of events, summarised in the song 'Over there, over there . . . The Yanks are coming. . .' These troops landed here on 4 May 1944.

The American troops had probably travelled in comfortable Pullman trains from their base camps to New York's Grand Central station *en route* to the troopship. One wonders what they made of this scenario as, after getting off the boat, they trudged along the platform of Riverside station trying to find a seat in one of the vintage non-corridor coaches of a British train. If this was also their first experience of overseas service, the station's shattered roof was their first sight of a bomb-damaged structure. Evocative scenes for all ex-servicemen.

MARITIME HERITAGE

Looking across No 1 Branch at Gladstone Dock at the time when the war in Europe was drawing to an end. Workmen are busy repairing bomb damage to the end of the south transit shed, while in the background at what had previously been the Canadian Pacific berth the *Empress of Australia* can be seen. She was never released from Government service and remained a grey troop-carrier until she was broken up at Inverkeithing in May 1952. *S. Bale*

Left After being in action with Germany's last capital ship *Scharnhorst* on 26 December 1943, HMS *Duke of York* arrived at the Gladstone to be refitted for service with the Far Eastern Fleet in the war against Japan.

Below Looking east towards the head of the graving dock from the bridge of the *Duke of York*. Tucked under the port bow is the Dutch cruiser *Van Heemskerck*, while off her starboard bow is a lock gate under repair. Stores and equipment litter the place - a far cry from the earlier artist's postcard painting! The building in line with and beyond the cruiser's foremast is the workshop of the Overhead Railway, with the Seaforth station platforms to the right of it.

MARITIME HERITAGE

Another view taken at quayside level. In the right-hand background the cast iron bridge carrying the Liverpool Overhead Railway is a prominent feature.

The end of Gladstone's West Wall was a favourite vantage point from which dockers and servicemen could watch the progress of ships entering and leaving the port. To the left of the lighthouse at New Brighton can be seen the low silhouette of Perch Rock Fort on which were mounted the searchlights whose sweep illuminated the ships berthed at the Gladstone at the beginning of the war. In this view the *Duke of York* gets a final farewell as she proceeds on her way to the Far East, where she became the Flagship of the Eastern Fleet in the war against Japan.

MARITIME HERITAGE

On 28 June 1944 the last attack by a U-boat pack (using snorkels) was made on Allied shipping off Selsey Bill, when a convoy of our Liberty ships was the victim of a torpedo onslaught and three were sunk, the fourth managing to make port in a damaged condition. During the month of June 1944 no fewer than 25 U-boats were sunk in the English Channel and Western Approaches, and the German Group West terminated its Atlantic U-boat campaign. The Battle of the Atlantic had been won - at last.

Germany's final effort to break our Northern Blockade was by the use of large cargo-carrying submarines. One of these was captured and the rest were sunk. In May 1945 *U-532* was towed to the Mersey and entered the Gladstone for unloading. The cargo was mainly copper, rubber and wolfram, which was confiscated. As the submarine was towed in, dockers and servicemen crammed every vantage point to have a first look at what had been an unseen enemy.

5. THE POST-WAR ERA 1945-95

The sudden surrender of Japan left Liverpool's docks crammed with war materials that required disposal, so the busy scene on the Mersey continued. Gradually the Government released vessels from war service and liners were returned to their owners to resume commercial use. Orders for new ships were placed with British shipyards in order to take advantage of the expected post-war boom.

Southampton was, once again, back in operation as Britain's No 1 passenger port, and Liverpool was left with the pre-war liner *Britannic* and the post-war utility one-class *Media* and *Parthia*; the former was most beautifully restored in the old White Star colours. It was a great tonic for the port when Canadian Pacific announced that the company would base its entire fleet on the Mersey, and its three white 'Empresses' became a familiar sight on the river. The real boom came with the export drive and the docks became almost as busy as they had been in wartime. The Gladstone cleared enormous tonnages to Australia, but it was the Birkenhead Docks, and Vittoria

The first signs of the return to peacetime conditions were the lifting of blackout restrictions and the repainting in house colours of ships' funnels, although it would be some time before the ships would lose their grey hulls and superstructure. In this 1945 aerial view of the Gladstone Dock it is possible to discern that some of the vessels have repainted funnels. Recognisable are the *Mauretania*, *Britannic*, *Queen of Bermuda* and *Empress of Scotland*.

Wharf in particular, that held the individual record for cargo cleared through a United Kingdom dock.

Two very depressing incidents occurred on Merseyside during the 1950s. In 1953 the *Empress of Canada* was destroyed by fire while berthed at Gladstone Dock. In 1956 the 'Dockers' Umbrella' became nothing more than a memory with the closure and demolition of the Liverpool Overhead Railway. Once that famous railway line had gone, Liverpool never seemed the same again.

In the late 1950s an ever-increasing number of Third World countries began to industrialise and produce their own manufactured items. Outward cargo traffic slowly declined, while jet airliners enticed passengers away from the liners. Consequently many of the older docks lost their significance and were filled in.

An enormous scheme was commenced in 1953 to rebuild the entire Canada-Brocklebank-Alexandra complex in the hope that Liverpool would be able to take her place in future overseas trade. Such optimism proved unfounded and some of the modernised quays lie unused to this day, while some older docks now accommodate high-rise blocks of flats and, of course, the famous Maritime Centre at the Albert Dock.

Traffic in general cargo, with its old labour-intensive 'tween-deck stowage, was steadily replaced by 'containerisation', and the newly formed Mersey Dock & Harbour Company opened the Seaforth Estate in 1972. Here there are facilities for timber, grain, meat and edible oils in addition to the Container Berth, which can accommodate the world's largest container carriers. However, most of the docks on both sides of the river have lost their transit sheds and appear empty and forlorn. Added to this has been the decline in the British shipbuilding and repair industry, which has seen the closure of the famous Cammell Laird yard in Birkenhead. Gladstone Dock is now virtually a 'vestibule dock', as the Royal Seaforth Dock traffic has to reach the river via the great Gladstone entrance opened in 1927. Commercial activities in the North Docks include the import of coal for power stations and the export of scrap metal to the Far East. Gladstone Graving Dock is no more and now does duty as a 'roll-on' terminal for commercial vehicles to and from Northern Ireland. Part of Liverpool's North Docks has been declared a 'free port' and piles of ingots, etc, can be seen on the quays under bond waiting until their buyers are ready to make use of them.

Furness Withy decided to restart its Canadian service from Hornby Dock, and took delivery of two new ships to replace the two that had been sunk during the war. The new ships were the 7,430-ton *Nova Scotia* and the slightly bigger *Newfoundland*, and each could accommodate 632 passengers. Here the *Nova Scotia* is being pulled away from the Stage by tugs at the start of a transatlantic crossing in 1948.

The assignment of berths at Gladstone Dock became apparent as the post-war services began to settle down. No 2 Branch North became the terminal for the United States Line, and No 2 Branch South was taken over by the Shaw Savill Line. No 1 Branch North became the terminal for Canadian Pacific, while No 1 Branch South was given over to inward-bound liners of Alfred Holt's 'Blue Funnel' Company. The West Wall was used by the Federal and the New Zealand Shipping Companies, which were now part of the P&O Group. The Cunard White Star Line preferred to use Huskisson No 1 Branch. This view, looking east, of No 1 Branch shows three new Blue Funnel vessels berthed at the south quay.
Mersey Docks & Harbour Board

LIVERPOOL AND THE MERSEY

The necessity of improving the docking facilities at the North Docks had been realised for many years, and in 1937 it was decided to construct another river entrance lock to replace the long-silted-up Canada Tongue. The advent of the war again delayed matters, but early in the 1950s work was started on the new Canada Lock. It would be 450 feet long and 65 feet wide, capable of use by medium-sized cargo liners at all states of the tide. Part of the £20 million scheme to improve Langton, Brocklebank and Canada Docks, and opened by the Queen in 1962, it unfortunately came too late to be used to its full potential, as general cargo stowage was in decline and the less labour-intensive 'containerisation' was taking its place. This view shows an early stage in the construction. *Mersey Docks & Harbour Board*

Another improvement scheme for the Port concerned the safety of mariners. Liverpool, with its tortuous approach from the sea, strong currents and constantly shifting sand banks located in a part of the world notorious for the vagaries of its weather, presented navigators with substantial problems. Any assistance that could avoid hazards and prevent collisions would enhance the reputation and attraction of the Port. Accordingly a Port Radar Station, technically the most advanced at the time, was installed in 1948 at the north-west corner of Gladstone Dock. The Radar Tower, seen in this view, became a prominent Mersey landmark and achieved its purpose.

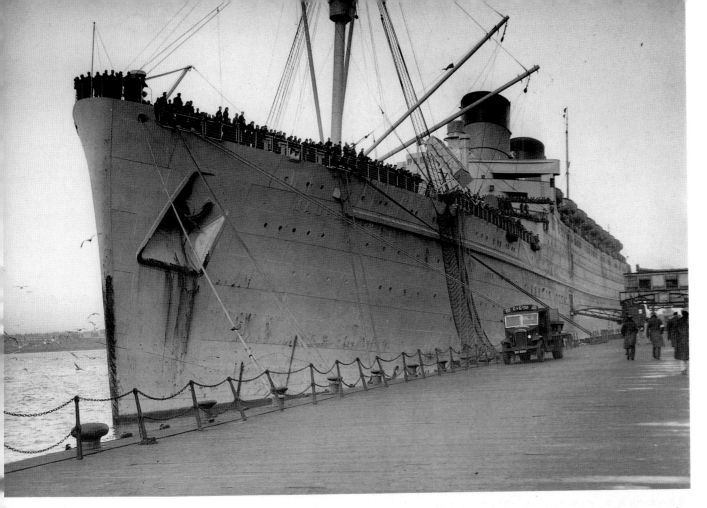

One of the first of the big liners to be released from Government service was the *Mauretania*. She is seen here at the Stage on 2 December 1946 discharging her last load of troops. After this she returned to her builders, Cammell Laird, for de-commissioning and refurbishment. Along the side of the vessel is the de-gaussing cable through which the electric current was passed in order to protect the ship from magnetic mines. The cable was removed during the de-commissioning process.

After a full refit at Cammell Laird, the *Mauretania* was back on the Liverpool-New York service, and made her first post-war voyage on 24 April 1947. After two voyages from Liverpool she was transferred to Southampton to act as a relief for the 'Queens', but when traffic began to fall off, due to air competition, she was refitted for cruising; she was made fully air-conditioned in 1957 and given a green hull in 1962. Cammell Laird did a magnificent job as a comparison with the previous photograph shows. Here she is about to set sail from the Landing Stage on her first post-war voyage to New York. However, her steam turbines made her an expensive liner to run, and she was broken up at the Firth of Forth on 23 November 1965. *Oxton Studios*

Left With Southampton back in business again as a passenger port, Liverpool could expect to offer only secondary services to New York. However, it came as a great tonic when Canadian Pacific announced that it intended to operate its entire passenger activities from Liverpool using Gladstone Dock as its base. A weekly three-ship 'Empress Voyager' service would be introduced as soon as the vessels became available.

The two 'Duchesses' that had survived the war, *Bedford* and *Richmond*, were renamed *Empress of France* and *Empress of Canada* respectively, and, after refits and being given white hulls, they joined the Flagship of the Line, the three-funnelled *Empress of Scotland*. The House Flag was displayed on their funnels. A call at Greenock was included in the service schedule. The *Empress of France* is seen here making an impressive debut in her new livery.

Below This busy river scene shows the *Ascania* at the Landing Stage with the Isle of Man boat ahead of her. The photograph was taken during the summer of 1948.

MARITIME HERITAGE

Cunard White Star announced its plan to run a weekly service to New York or the St Lawrence once the Government had released the *Franconia*, the *Scythia* and the last of the 'A' liners, *Ascania*. The White Star contribution would be the *Britannic* once she was ready for commercial service.

The *Franconia*, shown here, is best remembered for her wartime role as Churchill's Headquarters Ship at the Yalta Conference at which he, Roosevelt and Stalin decided on the unconditional surrender of the Axis Powers, the prosecution of war criminals and the formation of the United Nations Organisation to supervise the conduct of post-war international affairs. With her funnel restored to the company colours but with the rest still in wartime grey, this 1947 view shows her loaded with replacement troops *en route* to either the Middle or Far East. On the Stage a few cases and kit-bags have still to be loaded, while on the top roadway mothers, wives, fiancées and sweethearts wait patiently for the *Franconia*'s departure. In 1948 the vessel was de-commissioned and, after an expensive refit, returned to revenue-earning service for Cunard in 1949. *Oxton Studios*

After the war the first two new liners to be built for Atlantic service were the Cunarders *Media* and *Parthia*. They were large cargo carriers of 13,260 tons and carried only 250 1st Class passengers. The *Media* was the first British transatlantic liner to be fitted with fin stabilisers.

Many experts considered that the day of the battleship was over on account of developments in modern air power, but there was still one to come. HMS *Vanguard*, the last British battleship to be built, is seen here in Gladstone Graving Dock in 1949.

The 44,500-ton warship had a length of 814 feet, a beam of 107 feet and a draught of 35 feet, and she carried the 15-inch guns removed from the *Courageous* and *Glorious* when they were converted to aircraft carriers; her complement was 1,818. She had the most up-to-date anti-aircraft armament on any battleship afloat, with the capability of engaging 14 aerial targets simultaneously. Work on her construction during the war was periodically interrupted by the diversion of manpower to meet the more pressing needs for destroyers and convoy escorts, so she was not completed until after the war. She saw active service during the Korean War, afterwards being used for training purposes. *Mersey Docks & Harbour Board*

From time to time other major units of the Royal Navy were given refits prior to being placed in reserve. The *King George V* is nicely framed in this shot taken by a photographer leaning out of the carriage window of a Liverpool Overhead Railway train as it went past the Gladstone Graving Dock. *N. West*

Right In 1949 there was a serious fire in a cargo of latex rubber stored in Gladstone No 1 Branch South. The conflagration was quite spectacular and the pall of smoke drifting over the Port evoked memories of the Blitz in the minds of many people. Vessels in the vicinity had to be moved quickly to safety. After the fire had been put out, it took many days to remove the solidified rubber from the surface of the quayside, and especially from the grooves of the inset railway tracks.

Below There were many wartime cargo steamers built to a standard design in order to replace the losses caused by mines and U-boats. When the war was over these utility ships were bought up by various companies to replace the gaps in their fleets. Ellerman Line's *City of Ely* is a typical example.

In 1949 another well-known ship arrived back in the river. The *Georgic* was given her post-war refit at Newcastle-upon-Tyne and converted into a one-class emigrant ship taking people to Australia to start a new life, many taking advantage of the Government-sponsored 'Assisted Passages' scheme. The *Georgic* made a number of sailings between Liverpool and Sydney carrying cargo of hopefuls to a fresh start 'down under'. Though only a shadow of her former self, she was faithfully repainted in the old White Star colours before being finally scrapped at Faslane in 1956. *S. Bale*

MARITIME HERITAGE

Right The *Empress of Scotland*, Flagship of the Canadian Pacific Line, is seen here in Gladstone No 1 Branch fresh after her refit. On 9 May 1950 she made her post-war maiden voyage from Liverpool to Canada.

Below To enable the *Empress of Scotland* to reach Montreal like the other two Canadian Pacific liners, her masts had to be trimmed in order to pass under the Quebec bridge. The trimmed masts are clearly visible in this view of the vessel at the Stage. *C. Heywood*

Right In the immediate post-war period the Ministry of Transport operated a fortnightly troopship service between Liverpool and Hong Kong. One of the ships engaged on this run was the 16,500-ton ex-Anchor Liner *Cameronia* built by Beardmore in 1921. Although engaged in trooping, the *Cameronia*, seen here in the river, had her coat of wartime grey removed. The Ministry of Transport sold her in 1953 and she was renamed *Empire Clyde*.

LIVERPOOL AND THE MERSEY

Originally named *Letitia*, this Donaldson Company liner was used during the war first as a hospital ship, then as a troop-ship. With the cessation of hostilities she was not returned to her original owners, but was taken over by the Ministry of Transport, who renamed her *Empire Brent* and used her on the emigrant 'Assisted Passages' scheme to Australia. The Donaldson Company then chartered what was really their own ship from the Ministry of Transport for a number of trips to Canada. While under charter the funnel was painted in the Donaldson Line colours and the vessel was renamed *Captain Cook* in memory of the captain of the ill-fated *Athenia*; she is seen here in the latter role. She was finally broken up at Inverkeithing in 1960.

The *Britannic* was beautifully refitted by Harland & Wolff, almost to her pre-war condition. This picture shows her in the Mersey proudly flying the White Star pennant above the Cunard flag (as did her sister the *Georgic*). Those who remembered would wait until her monthly run came round in the sailing list before booking their voyage.

Britannic was usually fully booked after making her maiden voyage to New York on 22 May 1948, and she never came off the Liverpool-New York run until 1960, when there was a breakage in one of her crankshafts and she was repaired in the United States. Returning in the summer of 1960, with more passengers waiting to sail back to New York, the *Britannic* encountered the serious seamen's strike of the year and was berthed on Sandon West Wall waiting for the strike to end. Unfortunately her passengers were flown across by chartered aircraft and Cunard seized the opportunity to be rid of the last of the old White Star Line vessels. The empty liner sailed away under her own power to Inverkeithing and was broken up in December 1960. It really was the end of an era.

In 1948 the new 34,170-ton Cunard liner *Caronia* arrived at the Gladstone on her way from her builders, John Brown of Clydebank, and she is seen here berthed at the West Wall. Painted in the new Cunard green livery, she was expressly designed for dollar-earning cruises. Her maiden voyage from Southampton was on 4 January 1949, and she served Cunard well. In 1974 she met her end while under tow to shipbreakers in Japan, when she was wrecked on the island of Guam.

Noteworthy in this photograph is the outfall of the diverted Rimrose Brook on the side of the West Wall. The noticeable discoloration indicates yet further pollution of the River Mersey.

In 1953, despite indications that most travellers would now rather use air transport than sea - particularly in the case of travel to and from the United States and Canada - both Canadian Pacific and Cunard decided to replace their existing liners with more modern tonnage. Both companies could never believe that discerning people would prefer the restrictions of the airliner to the experience of a sea crossing merely for the sake of speed. As Cunard's Publicity Department put it: 'Half the fun is getting there!'

Two new 'Empresses' were ordered, the *Empress of Britain* from Fairfield's of Glasgow and the *Empress of England* from Vickers on the Tyne; both were sister ships of 25,500 tons, driven by steam turbines and capable of carrying 160 1st Class passengers and 1,890 in the Tourist Section. The *Empress of Britain* was the first fully air-conditioned British liner.

Cunard ordered three liners, with a fourth to follow a year later, all of gross tonnages between 21,300 and 21,900. All were steam turbine driven and were built by John Brown & Co. Their names were *Saxonia, Ivernia, Carinthia* and *Sylvania,* and each carried 150 in 1st Class and some 800 in the Tourist Section. They were all intended to operate from Liverpool, although the *Ivernia* made some voyages from Southampton.

Below Apart from the wartime Blitz and the post-war latex tank fire, Gladstone Dock did not experience many emergencies, but one truly spectacular one occurred on 25 January 1953 when the *Empress of Canada* was gutted by fire. So much water was pumped into her that she heeled over to port with her masts, funnels and superstructure caught against the quayside, thereby preventing her from completely capsizing.
The ferocity of the fire can be gauged by the scorched plates on her hull. The hosepipes snaking across the ship's side are connected to the Dock Board's fire tender *Vigilant.* Wisps of smoke are just visible rising from the bow section, while every window of the Overhead train passing in the background was no doubt crammed with spectators. The salvage operation for this 22,335-ton liner must have given the Dock Board engineers many sleepless nights, if not quite a few nightmares. *C. Heywood*

Above Following the disastrous fire in the *Empress of Canada*, Canadian Pacific had to find a replacement vessel for the coming season. The *De Grasse* was a 19,370-ton twin-funnelled liner built for the French by Cammell Laird in 1924. During the war she had been seized by the Germans, and as the Allies approached Bordeaux in 1945 the Germans scuttled her in an attempt to block the harbour. The French subsequently raised and completely refitted her, now with only one funnel.

When purchased by Canadian Pacific she was renamed *Empress of Australia*, the previous CPR liner of that name having been scrapped the year before. The new acquisition served CPR well for two seasons, and was then sold to Italian buyers in 1956. In 1962 she grounded at Cannes and was subsequently scrapped at Spetzia.

Below It would be 12 months before an attempt could be made to raise the *Empress of Canada*, and on 6 March 1954 the Dock Board faced its greatest ever salvage operation. No 1 Branch was cleared and, using experience gained during the raising of the *Matrona* in Bidston Dock soon after the war, A-frames were welded to the starboard side of the hull. Ships winches were secured to the roadway beyond the south transit shed and steam was supplied for them by hoppers moored in the Branch. Steel hawsers stretched across the basin and through the empty shed to the winches. Additional buoyancy was supplied by 'camels' strapped to the hull, and the *Vigilant* added compressed air. Gradually, watched by large crowds, the hulk became upright and the Board was able to repair and reuse a valuable berth. The wreck was taken to the graving dock and made ready for towing away to shipbreakers.

Above On 1 September 1954 the remains of the *Empress of Canada* were removed from the graving dock and towed out into the river where Dutch tugs took over the long haul to the breaker's yard at Spetzia in Italy.

Below left In April 1956 the new *Empress of Britain* arrived in the Gladstone, thereby releasing the *Empress of Australia* (formerly *De Grasse*). After embarking her passengers at the stage she set off for Canada, and this is a typical view of her gathering speed as she makes her way down-river.

Below Meanwhile the *Empress of Scotland* was laid up at the West Wall of Gladstone Dock awaiting disposal following the arrival of the new *Empress of England*. She was eventually bought in 1957 by a German concern, renamed *Hanseatic* and, after an extensive rebuild, returned to commercial use. After a serious fire in New York she was towed across the Atlantic for a survey in Germany, but the decision to scrap her was taken in 1966.

The Liverpool Overhead Railway, popularly known as the 'Dockers' Umbrella', closed on 30 December 1956. The rolling-stock was lined up at the Seaforth end of the line and stretched as far as Gladstone Dock, as this photograph illustrates. To many the Port was never the same after the Overhead was demolished.

On 2 September 1954 the first of the new Cunarders, the *Saxonia*, made her maiden voyage from Liverpool to Canada.

Astern can be seen the PSNC liner *Reina del Pacifico*, at this time nearing the end of her life; her replacement was launched in 1956.

The replacement *Reina del Mar* is seen here, resplendent and dressed overall, making her way to the Stage to embark passengers for her maiden voyage. The 21,500-ton liner had been built by Harland & Wolff in Belfast and would be able to carry nearly 1,000 passengers in three classes. However, she did not prove to be a paying proposition on her intended route and was returned to Belfast for conversion for cruising in 1963. She cruised from Southampton under Union Castle Management until she was sold and broken up at Koahsuing in 1976. With the increase in the cost of oil, her turbine propulsion made her expensive to run. Coming too late in the fight against the jet airliners, the *Reina del Mar* could perhaps be best described as 'a ship too late'. *Oxton Studios*

MARITIME HERITAGE

The *Reina del Mar* with tugs alongside is ready to sail on her maiden voyage. Ahead of her is the *Aureol*, which eventually acquired the sad distinction of being the last liner to leave Liverpool on a scheduled passenger service. Worthy of note is the

Riverside station roof, now repaired after sustaining considerable bomb damage during the Blitz. *Oxton Studios*

111

The old *Empress of Scotland* was replaced by a new ship, the *Empress of England*, sister ship to the *Empress of Britain*, and here the *Empress of England* is alongside the Landing Stage. The Pier Head in Liverpool's 'front door' and as such is one of the finest in the world, arguably only matched by the splendour of the skyscraper skyline of New York, and Sydney's Bay and Harbour Bridge. This photograph puts the Pier Head and Liverpool City Centre 'in the frame'. *Oxton Studios*

Above This rare view shows the two new sisters together in Gladstone's No 1 Branch, *Empress of Britain* nearest. The *Empress of England* sailed from Liverpool on her maiden voyage on 18 April 1957.

Below In 1959 an attempt was made to improve the *Empress of* *France* as a suitable running mate for the two new 'Empresses', and the old ship was given a cosmetic refit, the most noticeable exterior sign of which was the streamlined tops added to her funnels. To make way for the last new 'Empress', the *Empress of France* was withdrawn in 1960 after completing 337 round trips to Canada. She was broken up in December at Newport (Mon).

The new Cunarders were placed in service at yearly intervals and, by 1957, the fourth, *Sylvania*, made her maiden voyage from Liverpool on 5 June. These ships were so similar that Cunard might well have competed against the airline competition by placing them on a regular weekly service to New York, with special low fares that required the passengers to purchase their required food on board. Instead they were sometimes operating to Canada and sometimes to the United States, the *Ivernia* sailing often from Southampton. Unable to attract full bookings, they resorted to cruising in the winter months, but, with inadequate swimming pools and many cabins without 'en suite' facilities, they were not popular with Americans. In 1962 the *Saxonia* and *Ivernia* were taken off the Canadian service and given major refits expressly for cruising, being renamed *Carmania* and *Franconia* respectively.

On 13 October 1967 the *Carinthia* made the last sailing to Montreal for Cunard and was then laid up; Cunard's connection with the St Lawrence ceased.

The remaining liner, the *Sylvania*, was placed on the New York service and is seen here, unusually, in Gladstone Dock. On 24 November 1966 she made the last voyage between Liverpool and New York for Cunard, thus ending a tradition that was over 100 years old. Given a white hull, the *Sylvania* was laid up at Southampton until bought by Sitmar, a Liberian concern. She was towed to Trieste on 6 January 1960 and given an extensive overhaul for cruising. Renamed *Fairwind*, she ran from Miami to the Caribbean. She is currently named *Dawn Princess*, and like her sisters, two of which are now Russian-owned, she is still sailing.

C. Heywood

114

Above The only large Cunarders to be seen now in the Gladstone Dock were the *Mauretania* and *Caronia*. Each winter one of these would have a complete refit in the graving dock; in this case it is the *Caronia*'s turn. *S. Bale*

Right The 9,400-ton *Columbia* ran from Liverpool to Quebec for most of 1957 until she had a serious fire at that port, following which she was laid up at Piraeus and scrapped at Nagasaki in 1959. She had been built by Harland & Wolff as long ago as 1907, was named *Katoomba* and was kept mainly on the Australian trade. After the Second World War she had been given oil-fired boilers and manned by German officers with a Greek crew.

LIVERPOOL AND THE MERSEY   115

Cammell Laird replaced the *Ark Royal* sunk in 1941 with another aircraft carrier of the same name, commissioned in 1955. She was just as impressive as her predecessor with a length of 720 feet, beam of 112 feet, and draught to Flight Deck height of 86 feet 2 inches - one wonders how vital were the last 2 inches! She had a gross tonnage of 49,416 and could maintain a speed of 31 knots. The new *Ark Royal* used the Gladstone Graving Dock for hull inspections and repainting.

During the Falkland Islands Campaign her aircraft played a crucial role in the successful conduct of the conflict, and she did a bit better than her predecessor by managing to avoid the attention of lurking submarines and keeping out of the range of hostile aircraft. *Cammell Laird Archives*

Left and opposite page The last passenger liner to be built on Merseyside was the 1960 *Windsor Castle*. She was the largest passenger liner to have been built in England since the war, with a gross tonnage of 27,000 tons, and is seen here leaving Cammell Laird's basin, from where she sailed direct to Southampton for graving dock attention and her maiden voyage to South Africa in the Union Castle Line Fleet. The *Windsor Castle* made 50 round voyages to Cape Town without delay or mishap, and when the jet airliners took over she was not sold for cruising. Instead she became a floating hotel at Jedda, renamed *Margareta L*, and has been laid up at Piraeus in Greece for the last five years awaiting a buyer. *Both Oxton Studios*

MARITIME HERITAGE

Left The new 27,280-ton *Empress of Canada* was another liner that arrived too late to run profitably on the Liverpool-Canada service. Turbine-driven and built by Vickers at Newcastle-upon-Tyne, she could accommodate 200 1st Class passengers and 850 in Tourist. Her maiden voyage from Liverpool commenced on 24 April 1961, but it was soon found that the Canadian service could no longer support three ships. The *Empress of Britain* was sold to the Greek Line and refitted at Genoa in 1965 to be renamed *Queen Anna Maria*. In December 1975 she was sold to the Carnival Cruise Line of Panama and as such is still in service.

In December 1968 the *Empress of England* and *Empress of Canada* were both painted in the new 'Can-Pac' colours. The two-ship service continued until April 1970 when the *England* was sold to Shaw Savill and renamed *Ocean Monarch*, making one voyage to Australia; she had been given a £4 million refit by Cammell Laird for cruising from Australian ports. She was withdrawn from service in 1975 and scrapped in Taiwan.

The *Empress of Canada* then maintained a single-ship service until 6 December 1971, becoming the last transatlantic liner to use the Mersey. She arrived at the Landing Stage for the last time on 23 November, then went to her berth in No 1 Branch, Gladstone Dock, and is seen there discharging. This is a unique picture of the ship, possibly the last ever taken, and illustrates that the Branch was still in normal use with the roof cranes in position and, on the right, Blue Funnel vessels discharging at the south quay.

The *Empress of Canada* then sailed to Southampton where she was offered for sale and laid up at Tilbury. She became the *Mardi Gras* of Carnival Cruise Lines, and still sails on cruises from the USA.

Middle left and left Two pre-1968 views of the *Empress of Canada* in the River Mersey.

As a result of increased dock labour costs and modern technical improvements, the traditional 'tween-decks stowage of general cargo was rapidly being replaced by 'containerisation'. Here one of the regular Federal cargo liners is seen loading in the tradition- al way for Australia. When the new dock estate beyond the Gladstone was completed, entrance would be gained via the north-west corner of Gladstone Dock, and the transit shed seen in this view would be demolished.

Above The last liner to use the Mersey on a scheduled passenger service was the Elder Dempster Line's *Aureol*. Her final voyage from Liverpool was on 16 March 1972, and thereafter she used Southampton. Today she is still afloat, but no longer sailing, being used for accommodating visitors to Jedda. The departure of the *Aureol* marked the end of a magnificent era for the Port of Liverpool in the annals of the world's passenger liners.

Below With the demise of the large liners the Princes Landing Stage was considerably shortened and converted for use as a terminal for the Isle of Man ferries. The platforms at Riverside station were filled in and the former train shed was used for the storage of cars awaiting transport to Douglas, Isle of Man; it was subsequently completely demolished. The Stage is seen here in its present condition with the pleasure steamer *Waverley* alongside. In the background is one of the new cross-river diesel ferryboats.

The rapid growth of 'containerisation' to replace the older forms of stowage, with their labour-intensive force of dockers and their associated restrictive practices, forced Liverpool to follow the trend, despite the high construction costs that such modernisation would entail. It would be some considerable time before the new Seaforth Estate, built to the latest requirements, would be ready. Accordingly in 1967, with our ship-repairing industry in decline, it was considered that better use could be made of the Gladstone Graving Dock. The last ship to use it as such was the appropriately named Blue Star cargo liner *Gladstone Star* on 21 June 1967. Thereafter the original dual-purpose basin, opened in 1913, was permanently flooded and a gantry to handle containers was built over it; it now became Gladstone No 3 Branch.

On 1 May 1968 the first vessel to discharge its containers there was the small 700-ton *Estramadurian*, chartered by Ellerman & Papyanni. For some six years the No 3 Branch became the North Docks Container Terminal until the new Seaforth complex was able to take over and provide more extensive facilities. Many of the previously modernised quays at Langton and Brocklebank in Bootle were seldom, if ever, used and eventually became fenced in as an extension of the Free Port. The No 3 Branch at Gladstone then became a 'ro-ro' terminal for ferries that carried commercial vehicles to and from Northern Ireland, operated by the P&O company under its 'Pandorian' scheme. Apart from this, the Gladstone's quays became, as will be illustrated, dumps for coal and scrap metal awaiting export to the Far East.

Right The Americans leave Gladstone Dock in 1967. *D. Whale collection*

Below The new dock was not officially opened until 18 July 1973, by the Princess Royal; it then became the Royal Seaforth Dock. An enormous £32 million undertaking of more than 367 acres, it had been commenced in 1967, and the basin was excavated to a depth of 40 feet, with a new river wall extension brought out further west than that of the Gladstone Dock. An entrance was cut in the north-west corner of the Gladstone wide enough to pass any size of vessel. The dock is of the open-plan type with sufficient width to enable the largest ships to turn, and berths with some transit sheds arranged round the basin. These are able to deal with cargoes of timber, meat, grain and, of course, containers. There is also an enclosed area for the 'Free Port', which has been subsequently extended to many of the other parts of the remodelled Langton-Canada complex. Once the new container berth was in full operation, the temporary arrangements at the old Gladstone Graving Dock were dismantled, and that then became Gladstone No 3 Branch. It was considered that the dock was essential if Liverpool was to compete with other ports in the future.

The first commercial liner to pass through was the 12,000-gross-ton Blue Star liner *Tasmania Star*, built by Cammell Laird in 1950. She is seen here with a cargo of meat entering the Seaforth Dock on 6 December 1971, with the *Brocklebank* at the stern. The vessels are decked all over to mark the occasion. *N. West*

U.S. Army surrender port base

"The United States Army was yesterday forced to abandon positions it had held in the port." Sounds like a communique from some Far East battle. But there was no fighting, no rearguard action and the withdrawal was a very peaceful affair.

The port was in fact the port of Liverpool and the ten man staff of the U.S. Army Transportation Terminal Unit (U.K.) Liverpool terminal were leaving their Gladstone Dock headquarters for an office in the city.

The Gladstone headquarters were two huts near the main gate and had been in continuous occupation by U.S. forces — at one time jointly with the R.A.F. — since the 1940s, mainly dealing with supplies for the Burtonwood airbase.

The Mersey Docks and Harbour Board, who need the site for their new container berth, gave the Americans notice and yesterday at a simple ceremony First Lieutenant Charles L. Pike, commanding officer of the unit handed over the keys to Mr Eric Lawson, estates manager of the Mersey Docks and Harbour Board.

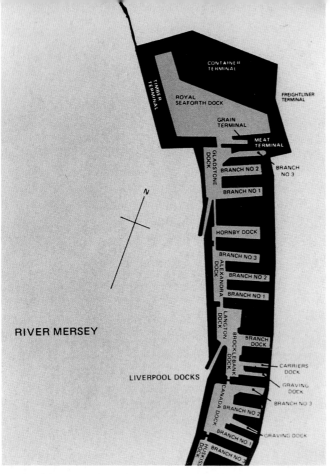

Left A plan of the North Docks today. Gladstone is now mainly a vestibule dock for the Royal Seaforth Estate; most vessels have to use the main river entrance opened in 1927. In the former graving dock the caisson has gone together with the pumping station. The only sizeable dry dock left in the Liverpool system is Canada Graving Dock, opened in the late 1870s. On the Wirral side, at the now closed Cammell Laird shipyard, is the enlarged No 5 Graving Dock (857 feet by 95 feet), which was enlarged in 1962. Today a limited amount of ship repairing is carried out.

The proposed barrage across the river would have been situated just below the bottom of this sketch plan and, in addition to generating many megawatts of electricity, would have provided another useful river crossing. However, the clearances required for supertankers using the Tranmere Oil Terminal would have curtailed its length somewhat, and the plan was abandoned.

The main activity at the north end of Bootle's Docks is the import of coal for power stations and the export of scrap metal to the Far East. There are many acres of unused quays and these form part of the 'Free Port', where goods are stored 'under bond' until required for manufacture. Much of the dockland is now a restricted area, and no longer can one roam its quays and bridges to look at the shipping, as the author did on his bicycle as a boy. Today a special pass is necessary. *Mersey Docks & Harbour Board*

Below Looking west from Seaforth across the expanse of the new Royal Seaforth Dock, the extent of the sea wall into the river channel can be plainly noted. On the left are the meat and grain berths, and beyond them is the entrance to the once famous graving dock, new designated Gladstone No 3 Branch. *Mersey Docks & Harbour Board*

Looking eastward across the Royal Seaforth Dock; a loaded container carrier appears ready to sail from the timber berth. The new entrance from Gladstone at the north-west corner (right of the photograph) will be noted, with the disused Radar Tower still evident. A new Port Radar Station has been built further north at Seaforth. To the right of the new entrance lie Gladstone Nos 1 and 2 Branches with their transit sheds bereft of their roof cranes. *Mersey Docks & Harbour Board*

This final sequence of photographs shows the docks today. The first shows the recently filled in Hornby Dock, once the haunt of ships belonging to the Furness Withy and Ellerman Papyanni Lines. Once the work is finished this area will be used for the storage of imported coal. Many an old mariner must be turning in his grave. *G. Parry*

Gladstone No 1 Branch - the final remaining part of the once well-known transit sheds. Coal is stored to the left of the remains of the shed. *G. Parry*

Looking to the west, we can see the disused Radar Tower surrounded by mountains of scrap metal awaiting shipment to the Far East by bulk carrier. Almost all trace has gone of the dockside sheds alongside which Federal liners once loaded for Australasia. *G. Parry*

MARITIME HERITAGE

Gladstone No 2 Branch has become the main quay for discharging coal. The large cranes load it into railway wagons for transportation to power stations in the North West of England. *G. Parry*

The new entrance connecting Gladstone Dock with the Royal Seaforth Container Dock. The new Estate can accommodate the largest bulk carriers and container ships currently sailing across the world's oceans. *G. Parry*

On the east bank of the Royal Seaforth Dock is the main container terminal. A large container ship is seen performing a quick turn-round unloading containers on to railway wagons. It is hoped that this facility may well be a salvation for Merseyside because, by using the Channel Tunnel, containers could reach EC countries more quickly and efficiently compared with the long haul via the English Channel and the North Sea.

Liverpool may yet become Europe's 'Gateway'. *G. Parry*

The *Queen Elizabeth 2'* did not sail up the Mersey until 24 July 1990 when she made a day visit to Liverpool. The significance of the occasion was not lost on the local population, over one million of whom lined the banks of the Mersey to witness the spectacle. Appropriately, at the helm was Captain Robin Woodall, whose home is in Hoylake, Wirral. As he approached the estuary he could not understand why the sandy shores at Formby and Crosby on one side of the river and at New Brighton and Moreton on the other were black until he looked through his binoculars and saw that they were crammed with people. These photographs show the *QE2* at anchor in the river, with the Merseyside Passenger Transport Executive's ferryboat *Woodchurch* acting as a tender for the last of the great transatlantic passenger liners and the largest passenger liner ever to come to the Mersey. *C. Heywood*

EPILOGUE

There have been several schemes to revitalise Liverpool's trade and commerce. A great barrage was planned across the Mersey just south of the new Canada entrance. This could have generated many megawatts of electricity making use of the fast-flowing ebb tides, but this idea was shelved when it was announced that super-tankers would once again use the Tranmere Oil Terminal. This required a much larger passage through the barrage than would have been required to meet the needs of the Manchester Ship Canal traffic and it was decided that the scheme would no longer be viable.

The improvement to Princes Dock entrance soon after the war brought forth the proposal to develop the site as a super terminal for Irish traffic, but the ferries are now too large to pass through the entrance from the river. Currently there is a proposal to construct such a terminal on the Birkenhead side of the river.

The most hopeful suggestion of all, now that the Channel Tunnel is completed, is the improvement of rail facilities to the Royal Seaforth Estate, enabling deep-sea ships to terminate their voyages on Merseyside rather than the Great European ports. If this happens Liverpool, having surrendered its 'Gateway to the West', may ultimately become the 'Gateway to Europe'.

A final farewell and 'good night' from the *Empress of Canada*, the last passenger liner to use Gladstone Dock and to sail from Liverpool on a scheduled transatlantic service - the end of a remarkable era.

INDEX